SAWED-OFF JUSTICE

SAWED-OFF

JUSTICE

by

Lynn Franklin

with

Maury Green

G. P. PUTNAM'S SONS   NEW YORK

Copyright © 1976 by Lynn Franklin and Maury Green

SBN: 399-11813-6

Library of Congress Cataloging in Publication Data

Franklin, Lynn.
  Sawed off justice.

  1. Franklin, Lynn. 2. Detectives—California—
Beverly Hills—Correspondence, reminiscences, etc.
I. Green, Maury, joint author. II. Title.
HV7911.F73A37   1976   363.2'092'4 [B]   76-19921

*All the events described herein actually happened, but many of
the names have been changed to protect both the innocent and
the guilty.*

*Dedicated to my father and mother,
who lived proudly in a time when
a thief was called a thief and not "sir."*

Contents

SAWED-OFF JUSTICE

1

Zip Code Number $$$$$

THERE IS nothing like Beverly Hills anywhere else, thank God! One planet couldn't afford two of them. It's a very small, very private city of about seven square miles and 35,000 people, most of them movie and television stars and their lawyers and other groupies, completely surrounded by envy.

Nobody ever heard of Beverly Hills until Douglas Fairbanks, Mary Pickford and Charlie Chaplin moved out from LA. Those three were the only upper class that Beverly Hills ever had. When they moved here, everybody else in the motion-picture business moved here, too, and the working classes followed—the chefs, chauffeurs, jewelers, hairdressers, clothiers, writers, real estate salesmen, interior decorators, accountants, lawyers, gofers, bodyguards, con men, thieves and other hangers-on. They all work in Beverly Hills except the stars, who don't do much work anywhere, but not many of the groupies except the lawyers and accountants can afford to live here.

Which is funny, because Beverly Hills is one of the worst credit-risk areas in the United States, except maybe Hamtramck during an auto workers' strike. You can get an

American Express card quicker if you live in Appalachia. Or Watts.

Beverly Hills looks a lot richer than it is. The real California money is in San Marino and Hillsborough, but that's quiet money. All the money in Beverly Hills is loud money. When there was no limit on political campaign contributions, guys in San Marino were chipping in fifty grand while the major studio bosses living in Beverly Hills never came up with more than about $300. They couldn't see the point in putting it where it didn't show.

Beverly Hills *makes* good money, but it doesn't *have* it. What we do have is the cream of the con artists, like the guy I handled for neglecting his kids. He lived in a house on North Bedford Drive that he leased for $900 a month. He had an executive job, a wife, four kids, a Spanish-speaking maid who lived in, and every year he took his wife away on a month vacation.

I got a call from a neighbor—neglect of the kids. I went out, and I found the maid feeding those four kids on crackers and peanut butter. That's all they had for a week. The guy and his wife had gone on vacation, and he left the maid just $100 to feed herself and those kids for a whole month.

We called in the social workers, and they found that the son of a bitch made only $1,400 a month. He had that $900-a-month house so that he could bring people out and impress them and pour them a drink and close a deal, while his kids lived on crackers and peanut butter.

That guy is typical of this town. Whatever anybody in Beverly Hills has is all up front. It's parked in front of the house, or it's on the finger or around the neck, where everybody can see it.

That makes trouble for me because somebody is always trying to rip that stuff off. I'm a detective. I work for the Beverly Hills Police Department. It's never called the BHPD, the way the LA department is called the LAPD. It's always full dress—the Beverly Hills Police Department. If that doesn't clue you, nothing will. It's a damned good department, with maybe 25 tough, smart, hardworking, almost unbeatable guys on a force of a 105, which is a fantastic percentage. Try it on your own hometown police force if you don't believe it.

The big trouble with Beverly Hills, from a cop's point of view, is that the merchants run the town. The city councilmen and the mayor are all part-timers, merchants mostly, and you can tell who's in charge by the layout of the offices in City Hall.

The Beverly Hills City Hall looks like something that was built about 1521 in Monaco, or Graustark, and imported by William Randolph Hearst stone by stone in the 1920s. Its style is a kind of vague Mediterranean, with a blue and gold dome and a big lawn with palm trees. On the first floor are the City Council chamber and most of the police offices. The jail is on the second floor. And on the third floor is the mayor's office. Detectives are in the basement. The mayor is on top, we're on the bottom, and the chief of police is in the middle, more ways than one.

The movie and television people don't give a damn how the town is run as long as they don't get mugged, which we see to it they don't, and the city officials go home at night, lock themselves into their ivory towers and couldn't care less what happens on the streets. So everything is run for the benefit of business on Wilshire Boulevard. When we need ten men for a stakeout, the mayor and the Council will make us put those ten men on traffic to keep the customers happy. With the loot covered by insurance, nobody but the insurance company cares.

It happens all the time—it happened to me many times when I was on uniform patrol—you try the door of a jewelry store at two o'clock in the morning, and it's not locked. You can just walk in. Now you have to call the station and see if they have an emergency number for the owner and get the dispatcher to call him and wake him up.

"Oh, my God!" the guy says. "I forgot. I guess it just slipped my mind."

"Well," the dispatcher says, "you'd better go down and lock it up."

"Look, Officer," the guy will say almost every time, "can't the officer who's down there secure the place, so I don't have to get out of bed and go down there myself?"

They *really* don't give a damn.

One or two of them set up their own break-ins. They'll deliberately set off the burglar alarm system two or three times for a month before the actual break-in. Every time we get several alarms like that from some of those big timers, we start watching the place because we know he's getting ready for a setup.

Half the jewelers in Beverly Hills break the law all the time. You can go in, pull off a ring or watch and say, "What'll you give me for it?"

They'll buy it. They'll take it in the back room, look it over and come back out and lay the cash on you. Checks are never involved, just cash right out of the pocket. Most of the stores have permits to buy used jewelry, which is required by law. But even if they have the permit, usually they forget to file the required document on the purchase. Most of them could lose their licenses twice a week for breaking the law, but nobody loses a license in Beverly Hills.

The town is run like a private club. Not everybody is a member of the club. But anybody who *is* sooner or later makes trouble for the cops. Like our ex-mayors.

About twenty years ago Edward Wharton had the job for one year. And for the next ten or twelve years, until he died, he drove around with a windshield sticker that identified him as Mayor Edward Wharton.

He had been out of office ten years when he ran a red light at Crescent and Sunset, in front of the Beverly Hills Hotel. He sailed through that intersection with no regard for the light at all, and he almost caused a wreck. I pulled him over.

He got out of his car, all jokes, and when I asked for his driver's license, he laid his card on me instead. It read: "Mayor Edward Wharton."

I looked it over and said, "Mayor Wharton, I don't know you, sir."

He snorted and said, "Mayor Wharton of Beverly Hills."

I said, "Mr. Freeman is the mayor of Beverly Hills. Mr. Jack Freeman."

"Oh," he said like he had forgotten, "that's right. Jack is the mayor now. You know we alternate."

He had the job once, for one year, ten years before, and now he says they alternate! So I gave him a ticket.

He complained to Clinton Anderson, who was the chief of police then, about my disrespectful, belligerent attitude and how I wrote him up for a trifling little borderline violation. The chief called me in and passed all this on.

"Chief," I said, "I wasn't belligerent, I wasn't disrespectful, but he told me a lie. He told me he was the mayor, and he's not the mayor."

Chief Anderson sighed and said, "Well, yeah, he tells everybody that."

Geoff Ducane is another case. He was the mayor so many times that it seems he is always the mayor. Evenings Geoff hangs out a lot at the Hideaway, in the Beverly Wilshire Hotel, and if the prostitutes in there just ignore him and go on about their business, the next day he calls in and complains about all the activity. He wants some arrests made.

What it really is, he feels neglected. Old Geoff doesn't want a girl; he just wants some attention. If a couple of the prostitutes flirt with him a little bit, we don't hear from him. I once told one of the girls, Lola Brown, who is one of my snitches, to flirt with old Geoff whenever she sees him, and it works like a charm—it keeps him off our backs.

Geoff is like all the other politicians when it comes to the city payroll. All they want is to brag to the voters about how much money they saved. Geoff was the mayor who laid a heavy gripe on Chief B. L. Cork a couple of years ago when the city was negotiating raises and benefits. Geoff used me as an example to try to hold down everybody's pay because the previous year I had made more money than anybody in the police department. The reason was that I spent the whole year living undercover with a bunch of thieves, the Red Velvet Gang, and I worked as much overtime as regular hours.

"I'm going to tell that bastard off!" I told Cork. "Hell, last year I kicked my way through more goddamned doors than he legally walked through. I'll ask him if he'd like to do that for the money I made."

"Hold it!" Cork said. "You stay away from old Geoff. I'll pass the word upstairs."

We heard no more from Geoff on that subject. Our politicians are just like everybody else's.

Another thing about Beverly Hills that is like most other towns: There is a right side and a wrong side of the tracks. The Southern Pacific runs right through the middle of town, alongside Santa Monica Boulevard. Every now and then they run a little train over those tracks, real slow, but that doesn't happen very often, and mostly people forget that the railroad is there. They think of Santa Monica Boulevard as the dividing line.

North of the boulevard the garbage is not allowed to smell. The hills in Beverly Hills are north of the boulevard, and so are the celebrities. Richard Nixon lived up there for a while, in Trousdale Estates. It's the part of town where a house that costs only a quarter of a million dollars is a blight on the neighborhood. There are more diamonds in those hills than in South Africa, and for every diamond there's a thief I've busted.

South of the boulevard is the wrong side of the tracks. Sam Goldwyn once said he wouldn't be caught dead living there. During one city election Geoff Ducane called everybody south of the boulevard a "bunch of drunks," which raised some pretty hell because Judge Andy Weiss and a lot of prominent people live on the wrong side of the tracks.

They all have trouble parking at night. Under a local ordinance, nobody can park more than thirty minutes on any public street in the early-morning hours. That thirty minutes is to give a guy time to bring his date home and kiss her at the door without getting a ticket.

The ordinance is citywide, but ever since I've been a policeman—twenty years—*all* the overnight parking tickets are written in the south end. There are *never* any tickets north of the boulevard. It's understood that you don't cite those people; you just hang a warning on them. They have 300-foot driveways and multiple car garages, and they need street parking about as bad as they need food stamps. In the south end there are a lot of old apartment buildings with maybe five garage spaces for twenty units, and the people really don't have anyplace to put their cars.

You can drive through Beverly Hills at two o'clock in the morning, and from Santa Monica Boulevard south to Whitworth, which is the city limits, there's not a single car on the streets. As soon as you cross Whitworth into LA, they're bumper to bumper. Those are Beverly Hills cars. The people park them overnight in LA and then walk back home into Beverly Hills. They're the affluent underprivileged.

My first contact with Beverly Hills was on the wrong side of the law. In 1940 I was in basic training at Fort Ord, and I came down to Hollywood one weekend with a part-time actor, Bart Snyder, who was also in basic. We met a couple of good-looking telephone operators, and we went riding around in Bart's car, a two-door single-seat Packard coupe. Bart and his date were up front in the car, and my girl and I tossed a blanket in the trunk, crawled in and slammed the lid on ourselves.

We were cruising around late at night having a good time,

and it was real cozy in that trunk until suddenly the car stopped and the lid popped open. Red lights were flashing all over the place. The Beverly Hills police had pulled us over.

They didn't know whether my girl and I had been kidnapped, or the four of us were planning a burglary, or what kind of caper it was. They FI'd us—made out field interrogation cards with our names, addresses, the license number, any useful information. And they raised a little hell with us and sent us on our merry way.

That was the one and only time I was ever in Beverly Hills until I applied for a job on the police force. By then it was 1955, and I was thirty-three years old, and I had been around a bit.

If anyone got me interested in law enforcement, I guess it was my father. He spent a year in prison, and I'm proud of him for it.

It happened when I was a kid of only five or six. My Grandmother Minnie got sick, and the doctor told my father that a whiskey toddy would do her some good. A slug of whiskey in sugary hot water was a common remedy in those days, the universal antibiotic of the era.

This was during Prohibition, and whiskey wasn't legal. Not that that made much difference in our part of Mississippi. Pontotoc County was pure moonshine country. So my father picked up his jug and went out to pay a visit to some friends who were working a still. He took Snowball, the bastard bulldog that I grew up with, and he took his shotgun; my father never went anywhere without his shotgun.

Just as he got to the still, there was a lot of whistling. The guys making the cookoff split, but my father just stood there. He hadn't done anything illegal. And the revenuers closed in on him.

Snowball, who had naturally picked up the general dislike of the feds that prevailed in Mississippi, started snarling and acting mean, and one of the revenuers said, "I'll kill that goddamned bulldog!"

My father squared off in front of the guy and said, "You kill the bulldog and you die next."

The fed backed off. But they took my father into custody, and when they got him into the jail in Pontotoc, the agent in charge made him an offer that he could refuse.

"We got you on being at the location of an illegal whiskey operation," the agent said. That was a crime in those days, just to be there; they believed in guilt by geography. "But I don't hold anything against you," the agent said. "It's the guys doing the cookoff I want."

My father didn't say anything.

"So now," the agent said, "I'd be much obliged if you'd let slip who they are."

My father didn't let slip anything.

"They friends of yours?"

"I don't know them," my father said.

"Then how come you were out there?"

"I was looking for squirrel."

The agent picked up my father's jug, which he had as evidence. "You catch squirrels in a jug?" he asked.

"No," my father said, cool as cucumber. "Usually I stomp 'em to death. But first I have to catch 'em, which takes some running up and down trees, and that gives me a powerful thirst. I carry a jug to quench it."

For some reason the agent got annoyed. "You son of a bitch!" he said. "You give me those names or you go to Parchman!"

My father said, "Point me toward Parchman."

They sent him up for a year, guilty of loyalty. The family moved down near the prison at Parchman. My father became a trusty, and he and the prison superintendent became real good friends.

And all during the year that my father was serving his time, he could come home and visit the family anytime he

liked, day or night. He had complete freedom to go anywhere he wanted, which was unheard of in those days.

They sent my father to prison, but they treated him like
the man he was. I'll always be proud of him.

Another guy who taught me something was my army
captain, Clyde Thornhill. He was about six feet four, 225
pounds, West Point, a rifleman to knock out a squirrel's eye
and a balls-out soldier. He was from Mississippi, too.

I went home to Pontotoc on a thirty-day leave, and I forgot to go back on time. I woke up one day and realized that I
was due back that day at Fort Ord. No way.

I went down to one of the local stills and bought two
quart fruit jars full of moonshine, and I took them back to
California on the train. I got there four days AWOL. I
walked in to the first sergeant, and before he could open his
mouth, I said, "I got to see the captain."

"Yeah," he said, "you sure as hell do."

I went on into the captain's office. I opened up my suitcase, and I put those two jars on his desk. "Captain," I said,
"I'm a couple of days late."

He said, "What did you make, bad connections?"

"A little," I said.

"Well," he said, "that's the way the trains are. You know,
there's a war going on."

I fought under that guy in North Africa, Sicily, Italy and
France, and I'd go to hell for him today. Clyde Thornhill
taught me to respect authority. Not because he had it, but
because he knew how to use it. He would overlook things
that were not important, but when it came to winning or
losing, he wanted every goddamned thing you had, and
maybe more. He got it, too.

After the war I farmed strawberries for a while near
Gainesville, in Florida, but then I began to work my way
west, to California. I had liked it when I was at Fort Ord,
and I always figured I'd come back. But it took me ten years.
I spent a lot of years bossing a steel-laying gang—what they
used to call gandy dancers—out of Denver for the Burling-

ton Railroad. That involved spending more time than I liked in places like Cheyenne, where it's so windy that the blizzards are horizontal—the snow never falls there, it just passes through town.

By the time I got back to California, on a vacation in 1955, I knew that the railroad was not for me. I didn't mind the rough life, but I wanted to do something more constructive. I wanted to leave more of a mark than a straight rail that the next train would pull out of line. I was thirty-three years old, and my options were closing out; it was time to make a move or forget it. And more and more I kept thinking about law enforcement.

So I was lying on the beach at Santa Monica, trying to decide which department to go to. Everybody on the West Coast was recruiting; LAPD was hiring sergeants away from New York and paying them more as rookies than NYPD paid them as sergeants. I picked up the Sunday LA *Times,* and the Beverly Hills Police Department was advertising for men. "Beverly Hills," I said to myself. "That sounds like Hollywood!"

I tossed my application into the hopper, and I found out that the competition was going to be tough. Beverly Hills is a lot more particular about the policemen it hires than the people it lets live here. Seventy-six guys were taking the exams, and only five of us were going to get jobs. After each exam—written, physical, psychological—more guys got trimmed off the list, until finally ten of us were left. We went before Chief Anderson, and he questioned us.

"Uh-huh," he said to me. "From Mississippi, huh?"

I said, "Yep."

He said, "I used to gamble a lot in Mississippi. In Biloxi. They got a lot of pretty women down there, too. You ever been to Biloxi?"

"I sure have."

I was one of the five he picked, and I'm pretty sure it was that Mississippi Connection that brought me luck again.

Right away I began to learn a few things. First thing I

learned is that police work isn't anything like what they show on television. Most of those TV series are pure crap. They get into more car chases in an hour than the average cop sees in a lifetime, and every week they shoot up enough ammunition to supply the Chinese army for World War III. They fly around like international jet setters chasing criminals, when what we really do is use the telephone and the teletype because no departmental budget could afford those plane fares and hotel bills and all the overtime involved. They use fancy space age technology which looks impressive but doesn't actually do much good; the way we catch criminals today is the same way we caught them thirty years ago—by getting inside the criminal's mind and thinking at his level.

The first time I kicked a door in I learned about that. I did it the way they do it on TV. The case was a rape-robbery, and the guy we wanted lived in South LA, and we went down to get him. We knew he was in the place because we could hear his TV going. We all had shotguns, and we had the element of surprise; but we were uptight because this guy had a reputation for violence. Any cop about to kick a door in is uptight.

I kicked the door in, and the guy jumped up off a couch like he was propelled by a big spring.

I said, "I am a police officer." It was a stupid thing to say—I had a uniform on; anybody could tell that I was a police officer. "Sir," I said, "would you please stand against the wall?"

I'll never forget the way he looked at me. It was like I was Santa Claus. He knew that I had no experience and that I was not about to shoot him. So he dived headfirst through an open window, and he got away.

Every time after that, when I kicked a door in, I said, "Okay, you motherfucker! Get against that wall or I'll blow your goddamned head off!" It's the only language they understand. When you say "sir" or "please," they know they've got a pushover, and they have no respect for you.

Another phony thing about police work on TV is that the case always ends with the arrest. That's only the beginning. After you bust the guy, you spend weeks or months fighting a weak-kneed deputy district attorney, who is afraid to file the case for fear of spoiling his record of convictions; an unethical public defender or a dishonest defense attorney, who will commit perjury to get the guy off; and a defense-minded judge, who looks for every flimsy excuse he can find to kick the case out of court. If murder is the crime, you're lucky to wind up with a conviction for overtime parking.

It was the case of an assassin who tried to kill me that first made me realize that the American court system is a fraud against every honest citizen.

At the time I was working uniform patrol on Beat 9, which is the Restaurant Row area around Wilshire Boulevard and La Cienega Boulevard, and I was riding pretty heavy on a group of small-time hypes. A group like that will get together, maybe fifteen or twenty of them in the same pad, and every night two or three will go out and rip some place off to make enough money to support the whole group's narcotics habit for another day or two. Whenever anybody from this bunch came into my area, I would pull them over and hassle them and FI them.

According to the Supreme Court, you can't do that anymore. Stopping a guy just to check him out, they put in a class with trial by drowning. But those guys on the Supreme Court are not running the show, they only think they are; they have never handicapped me. There is no way that a cop can stay within the guidelines of the Supreme Court and protect society. It's only the new officers just out of the academy who run scared and go by the book. I'll pull a guy over for a traffic violation, and who's to say he didn't commit it? Maybe it's only an unsafe lane change, but nobody in this world can drive two blocks without giving me cause to pull him over. And once he's FI'd, he's not going to pull a job because he is the first guy you're going to come after. He has to go home empty-handed.

After a while the group on Beat 9 got frustrated, and instead of doing the smart thing and working some other area, they did the stupid thing and sent this Charles Balsam after me. I could never prove that was the reason, but a cop knows a lot of things that he can't prove.

Just three hours before he tried the hit, Balsam stole a car. His idea was to kill me, dump the stolen car, and there would be no way to trace the killing to him. I didn't know the car was stolen because it hadn't been reported, but I knew he was trying to get my attention. He kept cruising my streets, going in and out of alleys, anything to make me pull him over on suspicion.

Finally, I thought, *Okay. Let's see what you've got in mind.*

I pulled up alongside him on Wilshire near San Vicente, eastbound, and motioned him over. The son of a bitch reached down and came up with a snub-nosed .38 and fired it right in my face. But when he made that motion, I hit my brakes, and instead of blowing my head off, he hit the front doorpost, and the bullet ricocheted off.

I took after him down Wilshire and radioed for help. We got up to seventy miles an hour, and I was ramming him from behind. I punched the bastard over onto the wrong side of Wilshire and up over the curb, and he slammed into a power pole near Crescent Heights Boulevard and wrecked his car. He jumped out and started running.

I stopped behind him, rolled out and onto one knee, and I yelled, "Hold it, you black bastard, or I'll kill you!"

About ten feet away two guys had a trash can up in the air, ready to load it into an LA city trash truck. They happened to be black. They dropped that can and took off.

Balsam didn't stop, so I let him have five shots. One of them knocked him down, but he got up and ran into a sub-garage. It was dark in there, so I held one bullet back. I figured I'd corner him inside and kill him. But I couldn't find him; he slipped out some way.

I came back out into Wilshire and almost got killed by Ed Zenter and Pete Reindell, two of our men, who came through the Wilshire-La Cienega intersection side by side at 100 miles an hour. They couldn't stop, and they almost ran me down. Everything in Beverly Hills had rolled on my radio call for backup, and half the cars in LA. The chopper was airborne from Parker Center, and a freeway pursuit special had peeled off the Hollywood Freeway, ten miles away, and was already halfway there. When an officer calls for help, everything else stops.

We finally chased the guy down there in the neighborhood, and Roy Garrett, one of our guys, shoved him over the trunk deck of a new Cadillac parked there on Wilshire.

Frank Alexander of LAPD Wilshire Division came running up with a shotgun and yelled something, and Balsam raised up a little. Frank thought he was trying to run again, so he split the guy's head open with the butt of his shotgun, practically scalped him. Frank was running too hard to stop, and his gun went on and smashed the rear window of the new Cadillac.

Between what Frank did to him and what I did to him, Balsam was bleeding all over the place. I had hit him in the back of the head with one bullet, and it had come out the top. Later the doctor told me that Balsam would have been killed except that he was running bent over when I shot him; if he had been upright, the bullet would have come out between his eyes. Anyway, he lived.

The trash collectors finally came back and got their truck. They talked to Ed Zenter about two blocks away and wanted to know if it was all right. He said yes, and one of them said, "We're not about to go back there with that crazy son of a bitch shooting that gun." I couldn't blame them.

It took hours to find Balsam's gun. He had thrown it away, and we had a whole crew looking for it. I made out my reports and went home to bed. Anytime there is a shooting involving an officer, there is a lot of pressure to justify it. After a while Wayne Rutherford called and woke me up.

Wayne is a captain now, and chief of detectives, and a good friend of mine. But that time he really bugged me.

"Lynn," he said, "are you sure that the guy really had a gun?" They hadn't found it yet.

I said, "Wayne, when I'm in a better mood, you call me back. I'm going to hang up on you now." I hung up long enough to kill the line, and I took the phone off the hook and went back to sleep.

When I went into the station again, they had found the gun. Sergeant Doug Mathieson found it in a patch of ivy where I had forced Balsam toward the wrong side of the street. It was the same snub-nosed Colt .38 that he had pointed at me, and it had one spent cartridge and five live bullets in it. It had been stolen in an LA burglary seven years before, and the serial number had been filed off, which is a felony.

Wayne started to talk to me about it, and I said, "Wayne, don't talk to me about that goddamned gun. It doesn't exist, remember?"

We took Balsam into Superior Court for attempted murder of a police officer, grand theft auto, having a stolen gun with the serial number filed off—every felony charge we could lay on him.

All he got was grand theft auto. Nothing else.

And that's where I first began to realize that the court system is a revolving door. For twenty years I've handled professional criminals, and as fast as I've shoved them into that revolving door, it has pushed them back out on the street. That's the story of my life as a police officer.

2

Sawed-Off Justice

A SAWED-OFF shotgun is just about the most vicious weapon made. It's small enough to hide under your coat or in a paper sack. It's strictly a close-range spray gun, and at close range there is no way you can miss and no way anything you hit can live. It turns everything it touches to hamburger.

For this reason it is a federal felony to possess a sawed-off shotgun. But judges don't seem to understand that anybody—*anybody!*—caught with a sawed-off shotgun is a son of a bitch who has declared war on society, a criminal so irredeemable that he ought to be hung up by his balls in the interest of public safety. No further evidence should be needed.

Instead, the courts treat a guy caught with a sawed-off shotgun the same as a kid caught with a stolen bag of candy. I got an education about that the evening Bruce Campbell and I still call Seven Dog Night, when it seemed we kicked in half the doors in town.

It was about eight o'clock when we got the call—a robbery up on Carla Ridge. We went up, and there was this big

27

fancy house, all imported white marble in front and white
stucco behind, with black hand-carved double entrance
doors about eighteen feet tall, like the place was inhabited
by giraffes. It was a sample of the local style of architecture
known as Beverly Borscht.

The owner was Loyd Kenton, the movie producer and di-
rector, and he and his wife had gone out for the evening.
They left a Mexican maid and two kids, a boy about eight
years old and a baby girl.

A black guy had knocked on the big doors, and the maid
was crazy enough to open up. She hadn't been in Beverly
Hills long enough to know better.

"He had . . . *servilleta?*" she said, having trouble with
the language.

"Napkin?" I said.

"*Sí,* napkin. Paper. And he want to know where is some
place. I don't know. He go, and pretty soon he ring again.
Now is other man with him, and they push me into the
house."

They tied up the boy, and they made the maid lie on the
floor of the den with the baby and threw a blanket over the
two of them. They took money and jewelry and two television sets, and they left about thirty-five hundred richer
than they came.

The maid gave us a pretty good description of the guys,
one short, one tall, like Mutt and Jeff. And when she answered the door, she got a good look at their car, a big white
Cadillac convertible about as inconspicuous as Liberace in
a crowd of Hasidic rabbis. All this information helped, but
one of the guys got careless, which was a bigger help; careless crooks make smart cops.

"The note, the napkin," Bruce said. "What did they do
with it?"

The maid just shrugged. We looked, and Bruce found it in
a wastebasket in a bathroom. It was the kind of paper napkin restaurants keep in those little chrome dispensers, and

somebody had written a name on it—Debbie—and a telephone number.

We ran the number, and it came back to an apartment in Hollywood where the manager, Joe Bartoun, turned out to be an ex-con who hated cops and wouldn't give us the time of night.

"All you bastards want to do is bust her for a little weed or something like that," he said. "The hell with you!" He was just out of prison on a narcotics conviction, and those hypes stick together like last summer's tumbleweeds. But sometimes a little psychology helps.

So I said, "Look, Joe, we don't work narcotics; we work robbery. All we want from Debbie is information. She knows these dudes, and they roughed up some kids."

"Kids?" he said.

I said, "Yeah, an eight-year-old boy and a little baby, a girl."

He said, "Ah, them son of a bitches!" He looked Bruce and me over again. "Robbery, huh?"

I said, "That's all it is."

And he said, "Okay. She's in two-B. Debbie Plantain. Nice kid, but kind of, well, out of it, you know?"

"Out where?" Bruce said.

Joe thought a minute, and then he said, *"Out* of it! She thinks if a guy screws her, it's a big romance. Then she wakes up in the morning and finds out it isn't. And so the next night she goes out again looking for another guy with a hard cock, which she finds, and every night it's like that. She could make a lot of money if she charged." He leaned back on a little desk in what he called his office, and after a minute he said, "You know what?"

We just looked at him.

And he said, "She's kind of sad."

Debbie turned out to be about twenty-five pushing sixty, with brown hair straggling down past a long, plain, pale face, wearing one of those crinkly-cotton dresses that look like they've been slept in and probably have. She was not anxious to rap with us.

"Well, I don't know them myself, really," she said. "I'm new here. I'm from Fort Worth."

"Welcome to LA," Bruce said. He held the napkin up in front of her, and he said, "They got your name and number, but you don't know them?"

"Well," she said again. She began with "Well" every time she talked. "Well, the other night I happened to go into this soul food place on Santa Monica Boulevard, and these guys kept making passes at me. And, well, I was scared of them, and finally, they forced me to give them my name and my phone number, so I wrote it on the napkin."

If she wanted to pretend that was how it happened, it was all right with us.

"What are their names?" I said.

"Well," she said, "they said they're Sam and Willie."

"Last names?" I said.

She shrugged.

Bruce said, "Which is the big one?"

She thought about that for a while. Then she said, "Well, the big one is Sam."

We talked some more, hoping maybe we could get something besides those goddamned street names, and finally, she said, "Every night they come in there." She didn't seem to realize that meant she went there every night herself, associating with these guys she claimed to be so scared of.

"Okay," I said, "you won't mind if we go down there and you point them out to us, will you?"

"Well," she said, "I guess not."

We drove down and parked, and Bruce and I watched while Debbie went into the place, which was called Charlie's Soul. It was loaded with blacks, just a few whites. Debbie talked to the cashier and a couple of other people, and she came out.

"Well," she said, "they haven't been in today, but I found out where one of them lives."

It was an apartment house on Melrose Avenue, about halfway from Hollywood to downtown LA. And just around the corner, like a birthday cake in the street, that fancy big white Cad convertible was parked. We didn't have a license number, but it had to be the same car the maid had seen.

The manager was a woman, black, white-haired, very tall, very dignified and gracious, and very scared. "Sam?" she said. "A big guy, maybe six-four? That would be Sam Booker. What do you want him for?"

"Robbery," I said.

And she said, "I'd be grateful if you could get him out of my building. That man and his friend Willie scare me to death. I don't know what they do, but I can guess. I've seen guns in that apartment, and they come and go at all hours, and I'm afraid even to ask him to move out."

Bruce said, "What kind of guns?"

"Oh," she said, "all kinds. They don't even bother to hide them. One of them looks like a little short shotgun, and once I saw two pistols, and another time a revolver. I go up to collect the rent, and I'm scared to go in; there are always guns around in there."

We called for backup from LAPD, and we kicked in our first door for the night, and here were a guy and two girls sitting on a sofa watching TV. We went through the routine: "Freeze, you motherfuckers, or we'll blow your goddamned heads off!"

The girls were no problem, and neither was the guy. He was one big son of a gun, about the size and muscles of Joe Louis in his prime, and he was sitting back real easy with his hands locked behind his head. He kept sitting there like a black stone monument to TV watching; he didn't even take his eyes off the TV.

"Sam Booker?" I said.

He said, "Yeah, that's me."

"Where's Willie?"

"Willie?"

I kind of jerked my shotgun a little, and real quick Sam said, "Willie ain't here."

I left him to Bruce, and I went back on into a bedroom; Willie was not there, and neither was anybody else. But on top of the dresser was a sawed-off shotgun with a barrel like a pistol, maybe eight inches, and the violation is anything under eighteen inches. And there were three shotgun shells lying beside it. I took the shotgun, and I went back into the living room. Sam still hadn't even blinked an eye.

I said, "Is that your white Cad convertible parked downstairs?"

He said, "Yeah, that's mine."

"You got the keys?"

"Yeah, I got the keys."

"Well, let me have them."

"Okay," he said. But he still didn't move.

I said, "Dammit, Sam, where are they?"

"In my hand," he said.

"Okay, give them to me."

"Man," he said, "is it all right if I take my hand down?"

I said, "If you got the keys in your hand and you're going to give them to me, then you got to take your hand down. Right?"

And he said, "Yeah, but I been through this before. When the police comes busting in my door with shotguns and they yell, 'Freeze!' they mean *business.* I ain't *about* to move, you know?"

That was one wise con. But we got nothing out of him, and we got nothing out of the Cad. He and Willie had already fenced the stuff, and we never did make any recovery except for one TV set, which Kenton's insurance company had already replaced by then, which was many months later.

The landlady told us about another pad where maybe Sam's friend Willie lived, over in the Wilshire district, and we went over there and kicked in another door and got three guys, but no Willie. So we sent them on into jail to join Sam. You can't turn any of them loose until you've got the right ones, so you put them in the basket and shake them and see which ones come out.

One of these guys talked enough to give us another lead, so we busted in our third door of the night, and we got two more guys, back in the Melrose area, but still no Willie. Now we got six in the basket.

And one of them admitted to knowing Sam Booker, and from him we learned that Willie's real name was George McArthour. But nobody knew where George was.

So I picked up the phone and called one of my best snitches, Len Swinger, and I told him what I needed.

"George?" old Len said. "George McArthour, with an *o*? Lynn, I never heard of nobody by the name of George McArthour. You sure he's black?"

"Goddammit, Len!" I said. "His street name is Willie."

Len said, "Yeah, that's right. You told me about that."

"Look," I said, "what about that job you pulled in Downey last Friday night?"

"How'd you know about that?" Len said.

I said, "Len, I don't tell everything I hear about. I haven't had any occasion to make a call to Downey. But I might, if you don't tell me what *you* know."

"Yeah," Len said. "Let me think a minute." He thought for maybe three seconds. "Hey, man, I remember old George! Yeah, him and Sam Booker, they live together someplace on Melrose."

I was getting tired of this. "Len," I said, real hard, "tell me something."

"Yeah, tell you something. Yeah. Okay. Yeah. Well, there is this white gal up in Los Feliz. . . ."

This is a part of LA which Cecil B. DeMille developed

back in the twenties. It's at the east end of the Hollywood Hills, and the DeMille place is still there, and so is W. C. Fields' and a lot of others, and some expensive homes and new apartment towers and some crummy old places, and a lot of doctors because the Sunset Boulevard medical complex is about a five-minute downhill run.

This was in one of the old places, third floor, no elevator. That's as high as it's legal to go without an elevator in LA. Bruce and I climbed the stairs, and when we got outside the apartment door, we could hear that somebody inside was watching TV. I had my foot up to kick the door when I heard the TV dispatcher say, "Adam 12 and all units in the area, a 211 in progress. . . ." I put my foot down very quietly and held my gut, and Bruce and I stood there laughing and not making a sound until we could get ourselves together again.

When we were ready again, we went through that door like it was tinfoil, and here at last was our little man of the evening, Willie-George, sitting there staring at TV with a great big fat white girl twice his size. That had to be some remarkable kind of love affair.

It had been such a busy night that by now we were out of handcuffs, so as we went out, I told Willie-George, "You lock your hands above your head and walk down those stairs. And if you stumble, you son of a bitch, I'll blow your head off."

Bruce was leading the way, and he turned back and said, "Hey, man, if you start to shoot, tell me first so I can get out of the way. I don't want blood all over my clean suit."

And the fat girl, who was standing up at the top of the stairs watching us go, screamed down at me, "You dirty fucking fuzz! You can't talk to my friend like that!"

It was now maybe three o'clock in the morning, and my foot hurt from kicking doors and I was tired, and maybe I was tired of people like her before I was born, so I just turned around to face her, and I pumped one into the chamber, ready to go.

You never saw a scared fat girl disappear so fast.

When we finished shaking the basket, everybody came out. We made every one of the seven guys we busted on one crime or another, and even though we didn't recover the Kenton stuff, you'd think we'd have felt pretty good about Seven Dog Night.

The hell we did!

We went into Beverly Hills Municipal Court for Sam Booker's preliminary, and Judge Marvin Fang ruled that it was okay for us to bust in Sam's door, but that I had no reason whatsoever to enter that bedroom and confiscate the shotgun.

Judges don't have to explain their decisions, and most of them never do; they just act like they got them on the mountain. If they took the mystery out of it, the people would realize how little law the judges know.

It's my guess Judge Fang was leaning on a 1969 United States Supreme Court ruling in a case called *Chimel* v. *California*. It says partly, "There is no . . . justification . . . for routinely searching any room other than that in which an arrest occurs. . . . No consideration relevant to the Fourth Amendment suggests any point of rational limitation, once the search is allowed to go beyond the area from which the person arrested might obtain weapons or evidentiary items."

It's easy for Justice Potter Stewart, who wrote that opinion, to sit up there in his black robes and make rulings like that, but it isn't Justice Stewart who's going to get his ass shot off if Sam Booker's buddy is hiding in the bedroom. Cops who fail to secure the premises when they make an arrest don't usually live long enough to collect their pensions.

Besides which, if it was *Chimel* that Judge Fang followed, he was off the track anyway because there was no second suspect in the Chimel case, which was down in Santa Ana. Those cops didn't have to worry about getting bushwhacked.

So here we had a combination of a Supreme Court ruling so unreal it's weird and a Beverly Hills judge who can't read the law right.

When we got into Superior Court, we convicted Booker and McArthour of the robbery, but after Judge Fang threw out the shotgun felony charge, that whole Seven Dog Night's work just left a sour taste in my mouth.

But even that wasn't as sour as the case of Sweet Williams, Jr.

We had a bunch of afternoon robberies in Beverly Hills where the MO, the method of operation, was always the same. A young black guy, sometimes two or three of them, would rip off some elderly woman as she came home from shopping and drove into her garage. The guys didn't get a lot of money, but they got credit cards, which they used to rip off the stores. The victims didn't know weapons, but from what they told us one of these guys carried a sawed-off shotgun.

I wanted that guy bad. And after a while I got the word from Len Swinger that maybe the guy was Sweet Williams, Jr. I ran the name, and he turned out to be nineteen years old with a rap sheet that showed fifteen arrests, a guy who always drove a new Cadillac but never worked a day in his life. His girlfriend, who had a baby by him, clerked in a grubby hotel in downtown LA, and she also collected welfare checks. His story was that she supported him and his new Cadillacs.

Before I could talk to Sweet Williams, Jr., we had a homicide that looked like it belonged with these robberies. The victim was a sixty-four-year-old widow, Mrs. Edna Cartwright, who lived in an apartment on the east side of town just off Wilshire. She pulled into her driveway one afternoon, and a black guy parked at the curb walked up the driveway behind her, pulled her out of her car and stabbed her to death right there, in front of two witnesses. He stabbed her twenty-four times.

One of the witnesses was a neighbor, Mrs. Carole Spender, who happened to walk by and saw it all. But she didn't realize the guy was stabbing Mrs. Cartwright; she thought he was beating her.

"Let that woman go!" she yelled at him, the way she told it. "Turn her loose!"

And very politely the guy said, "Yes, ma'am," and he dropped Mrs. Cartwright to the pavement, walked back to his car, and drove off.

I showed Mrs. Spender a picture of Sweet Williams, Jr., but she couldn't make him as the killer. She had bad eyesight. "Could be," was as far as she would go.

The other witness was Mrs. Cartwright's son, Edward, who was thirty years old, a long-haired hippie just out of four years in prison for dope and high on the stuff again.

Edward was standing on the balcony of their apartment, on the second floor right above the driveway. When the killer walked back out to his car, Edward could practically have reached down and grabbed him by the hair.

But Edward was a creep who couldn't grab his own balls.

"You saw it all," I said to him. "What happened?"

"You know," he said, "I came out, I looked down there, and one of my robots saw my mother being beaten. And then the guy dropped her and went that way, down the driveway, and my other robot turned and looked at him."

"What did you do?"

He said, "I couldn't make up my mind what to do."

I showed him pictures, including Sweet Williams, Jr., and he said, "Oh, I wouldn't identify anyone. I might pick the wrong person."

So two witnesses added up to no witnesses. But I thought I could get Sweet Williams, Jr., on my robberies, and maybe if I could talk to him, he would cop out to the homicide. So I got some of the guys and went down to 77th Street Division LAPD, and they gave us backup, and we went to his house. I knocked on the door.

He opened the door in pajamas, and I backed him inside
and busted him, and we went through the required routine
about his constitutional rights, which is not news to guys
like Sweet Williams, Jr., because they all know their rights
better than any judge.

And he said, "Can I get some clothes on?"

I said, "Okay," and we went back to his bedroom. It was
all cluttered up with boxes of stuff and clothing and gadgets, like a radio and fishing tackle and weights for lifting
and every goddamned thing you can think of. It looked like
a pawnshop after a tornado. And I was looking for a shotgun.

I said, "Now look, Williams, do you have a shotgun in
this room? Tell me if you have, before I start moving things
about."

"Go ahead and look," he said.

I looked under the bed, and there was the sawed-off shotgun. I looked around some more, and most of the stuff in
the room was probably stolen, but not from Beverly Hills.
What I wanted, which I found, was half a dozen credit cards
and some jewelry from my robberies.

So we booked Sweet Williams, Jr., for robbery and possible homicide, and eventually we went before Judge Bradford
Service in Superior Court in Santa Monica. I testified about
the arrest and the shotgun and the other evidence, and
Judge Service said, "Tell me now again, exactly what you
said."

I told it all again.

And he said, "You meant, whether you had permission to
search or not, you were going to search, regardless of what
the defendant said."

And he threw out all the evidence—sawed-off shotgun,
stolen credit cards, stolen jewelry, everything—for illegal
search and seizure. Without evidence we couldn't make a
case. We lost, and Sweet Williams, Jr., won.

It's the only decision I ever heard of based on mind reading, which has about as much standing in a court of law as witchcraft. Judge Service knows me, and he was right that I was going to go ahead and search with or without permission, but that was only his opinion the way the law looks at it. He knows damned well he could only get away with that crap in a ruling against the prosecution; if he tried it against the defense, the case would be overturned on appeal.

Besides which, I had the man's permission to search, and the law says clear as glass that if I have permission, the search is legal.

But Judge Service ignores the law. He makes his own law.

I don't know whether Sweet Williams, Jr., killed Mrs. Edna Cartwright, but I do know he had a sawed-off shotgun, and I do know he committed a lot of those afternoon robberies. He told me so himself.

That was after my case was thrown out, when Hollywood LAPD took him over for investigation of some of their homicides. I talked to him afterward.

"You can talk," I said, "because my case is dead."

"Yeah," he said. "That sure is one cool judge."

"Okay. How about those robberies?"

He said, "Sure, man, some of them was me. We got a bunch of us goes out to Beverly Hills every couple of days, we cruise, we see some old woman driving by herself, we follow her home, she goes in the garage, we rip her off. It's easy stuff."

With guys like Bradford Service on the bench, making up their own law as they go along, it gets easier all the time. Sawed-off shotguns aren't half as big a problem as sawed-off justice.

3

Martini Justice

THERE'S ONE kind of perverted legal process that's good for nobody but criminals, and that's martini justice. The courts are full of it. You can see how it starts in any bar near any courthouse about four thirty or five o'clock in the afternoon any day court is in session. Just drop in, prop yourself up at the bar, and look around.

What you'll see is judges drinking with lawyers. Defense lawyers. Keep looking, and you'll notice that it's always the lawyer who picks up the tab.

The guy drinking with the judge is almost never a prosecuting attorney, and it is absolutely never a prosecutor who buys the drinks. The prosecutor is on the public payroll; his annual salary wouldn't begin to cover a successful defense lawyer's booze bill. The judge, who is also on the public payroll but a lot farther up, could afford to pick up the check, but it's beneath his dignity. Free drinks go with the office.

Besides, the judge is uncomfortable drinking in public with a prosecutor; it looks prejudicial to the defense. But drinking with defense lawyers is okay because the judge doesn't give a goddamn about the prosecution's rights. The

41

prosecution never appeals, and judges only worry about what might happen on appeal to make them look bad. Too many reversals, and the judge never gets a chance at the appeals bench himself.

So it's friendship and influence that decide many a case. Judges and defense lawyers drink together, they take their wives out to dinner together, they play cards together, and many places—Beverly Hills is one of them—they wear the same old school tie. Here in Southern California we get more judges out of USC than any other law school, but whether it's USC or Stanford or Harvard doesn't make any difference—it's still martini justice.

Which is more dangerous than the payoff, because you can get to a crooked judge, but you can't get to a judge who won't even believe you if you tell him he's basing his decisions on friendship instead of law.

Armand Zeller wouldn't believe you. He sits up there in Beverly Hills Municipal Court as imperial as God on the toilet, but you should see him bowing and scraping when Larry Warren walks into his courtroom. Judge Zeller doesn't realize how it looks.

Larry is a clever guy who handles most of the fags in Beverly Hills and around LA and a lot of other criminal cases, too. But you never see him in Beverly Hills in the morning; he is too busy downtown in LA, where there are a lot more courts and a lot more fag clients.

All four of the Beverly Hills judges set court call every morning at nine o'clock, which means everybody on that day's call is supposed to be there—the deputy DAs, defense attorneys, defendants, police, witnesses, everybody.

So what happens at nine o'clock? Nothing happens. The judge isn't there. Except in Leo Freund's court, which is different from the others—I'm not talking about him.

About nine thirty or ten o'clock the judge wanders out, and the clerk begins calling the cases. If somebody is missing and there has been no phone call or excuse made, what's supposed to happen is that if the missing guy is the defendant, the judge issues a bench warrant for his arrest, and if it's anybody else, the judge issues a show-cause contempt citation.

But not in Beverly Hills. In three of the four courts in Beverly Hills the clerk just puts the case file aside, and he calls the next one.

After about thirty minutes the judge declares a ten-minute recess and goes back into his chambers. I have never seen a ten-minute recess in those courts; it's the only place where ten minutes lasts at least half an hour. Then there's a second call, and a little more business, and it's time for lunch. In the afternoon it's more of the same.

All this time, while nothing is happening, a whole bunch of attorneys, defendants, witnesses, arresting officers, victims and prosecutors are sitting around waiting for their cases to be called. It's like waiting for the Second Coming.

About three o'clock in the afternoon Larry Warren rolls up outside in his chauffeur-driven limousine, and he parks in the red zone. If he gets a ticket, somebody will take care of it for him.

Larry strolls into court, and he always pauses at the door and looks around, like he's casing the joint. What he is really doing is waiting for the judge to notice him. Larry has a flair for the dramatic.

If it's Zeller's court, which is the worst, the judge will look tickled pink, and he will say, "Oh, I see we have Mr. Warren with us. Will you approach the bench, sir?"

Larry comes up, and Judge Zeller says, "What case do you have, Counselor?" Larry names a case, and the clerk pulls it from the stack of those that didn't show.

And Larry will spread a big smile and say, "Your Honor, if I could ask the indulgence of the court, I have such-and-such other cases." And the clerk pulls those, too, and the judge disposes of all of Larry's cases, like this was Larry's own personal judicial system. Idi Amin gets no better deal in Uganda. And now the judge actually *thanks* Larry for being so nice as to honor the court with his presence, Larry thanks the judge for his courtesy, and Larry leaves.

This is just a friendly thing, no payoff. Of course, Larry keeps a list of the favorite whiskey of every judge around, and every Christmas he makes sure that every judge gets a case of his favorite so that he will remember Larry kindly. But that's not a payoff; nobody buys a judge with a case of scotch. But it does help to keep things friendly. Too goddamned friendly.

By right, those attorneys who have been sitting around all day waiting for Judge Zeller to get his ass in gear should stand up and object. But nobody does. Nobody dares because if he did, he might get a bad decision. He can't be sure, but he is afraid that he might.

That's 100 proof martini justice.

Anyway, the only reason everybody has to wait around all day in most courts is the judge is incompetent or lazy or both. The crowded calendar they all blame is pure bull dung. Calendars are crowded because judges don't follow the law and the rules of court procedure, and some of them do no more work than a senile coon hound. The judges proved it themselves here in LA County, where the Judicial Council made a study and found that the average judge works only four hours and forty-three minutes a day. At that rate Rome wouldn't be built yet.

Where the judge really works and where he applies the law strictly, you can see the difference. Judge Leo Freund is called the "law west of La Cienega," and where he presides, the calendar is never crowded.

When Leo Freund says, "My court begins at nine o'clock," he doesn't mean one minute after nine. When he calls a case, anybody who doesn't answer is in deep trouble. Larry Warren will do anything to keep a client out of Leo Freund's court; it ruins Larry's whole day.

By noon Judge Freund has cleared his court and is order-

ing his lunch at his favorite country club, and his biggest
worry is fading his tee shot into that big tree on the first
hole. A lot of people call him a cantankerous old bastard,
but he lives the good life, and I wish him a lot of it because
he has earned it.

When you get a case of martini justice, the friend isn't always a drinking pal of the judge, and the consideration isn't
always a martini. There are other ways to influence a judge,
and sex is 200 proof.

The case that taught me that began the night a Ringo
Starr rock movie opened at the Canon Theater, and Ringo
was there in person. A rock audience always acts like a
bunch of apes that haven't been housebroken, and the
theaters have learned to buy plenty of security. So we had
two firemen on duty, plus six uniformed policemen and me
in charge in plain clothes.

About eight o'clock in the evening the manager, George
Newsom, came up to me backstage and said, "Lynn, we got
a problem."

"Yeah," I said, "I can smell it. But I'm not going to bother
with that."

"No, no, no," he said. "I don't care about the pot. But we
got a man wandering around the lobby with a gun. My pro-
jectionist."

"What's he doing with a gun?" I said.

George didn't know.

I said, "What's his name?"

"Marvin Hill."

"Okay," I said, "show him to me."

We went into the lobby, and George pointed into the
crowd, and here was this big skinny guy with a face like re-
boiled linguine, and a revolver butt was sticking out the left
front pocket of his blue denim safari pants, plus he had a
blackjack in the right back pocket. The sap was just plain
illegal, and there was no way he could have had a permit for
the gun; some of the cow county sheriffs up north give gun

permits to private citizens, but that doesn't happen in LA
County. This guy was careless about letting these weapons
show, which meant that he was some kind of nut, and he
was walking around in the middle of a crowd of several
hundred Starry-eyed kids half gone on pot.

While I was trying to decide how to handle this, Marvin
Hill took a long look at me standing there with George
Newsom, and he made me for cop. He took a quick turn,
headed for a stairway and went up the steps three at a time.

I took after him, but when I got upstairs, Marvin had
locked himself in the projection booth. The steel door had a
little window, and I looked in and Marvin looked back at
me like I wasn't even there.

"Okay," I said to George. "Now we wait."

"Wait?" said George. "What for? I wish you'd get him out
of here; he makes me nervous."

"Look," I said, "you got a theater full of people here, and if
I start to kick that door in, that crazy guy just might start
shooting down into the audience. We'll wait."

So we waited. Through the little window I could see that
Marvin was puffing pot, and George Newsom was chewing
his fingernails clear up to the armpit by the time the show
was over and we got the theater cleared. Then I had a couple
of the uniformed men stand behind me, where Marvin
could see them, and I put knuckles to the door. He looked
out the little window, and he grinned and unlocked the
door and came out, no trouble at all.

"You're wasting your time," he said when I cuffed him. I
thought he was just high on the weed, but it turned out he
knew something.

Besides the gun and the blackjack, Marvin Hill had that
projection booth loaded with every kind of narcotic you
could think of. He had a complete hype kit, heroin, cocaine,
pills, weed, everything. You could smell pot all over the
theater, but the air in that booth was sweet enough to bottle and sell at rock festivals.

So I took a whole bagful of stuff, and I booked Marvin on

everything. And all the time he just kept grinning at me. We drew Judge Zeller for a preliminary, and now we started getting delays. The defense attorney, Marc Mansion, kept asking for continuances, and Zeller kept giving them to him, and Marvin kept grinning.

"You look pretty happy about all this, Marvin," I said one day when I found him standing outside the courtroom in the corridor during one of those half-hour ten-minute recesses.

He held up two fingers, side by side, and he said, "Franklin, like I told you, you're wasting your time. The judge and my mother are just like that."

I can't prove that was it, but what happened after all the delays was that one by one all the narcotics charges got thrown out, and the concealed weapon charge got thrown out, and finally, nothing was left but possession of a blackjack. Judge Zeller let Marvin cop out to blackjack misdemeanor, Marvin paid a goddamned little $25 fine, and that was the end of it.

Marvin was right all along: I was wasting my time. Here was a guy who broke half a dozen laws, he was caught with the evidence, and his penalty was a fine that wouldn't discourage a penny-bank bandit. I don't know whether Judge Zeller was sleeping with Marvin Hill's mother, but I know who got screwed. It was the public.

Political clout makes for another kind of martini justice. My detective partner, Bruce Campbell, and I got a taste of it the time we busted the nephew of the mayor of one of the cities in LA County. We sprout cities around here faster than a thief thinks up alibis; at last count I think we've got seventy-seven.

What happened was two guys snatched a purse from an old lady on Roxbury just off Wilshire, and we caught both of them five minutes later. They had thrown away the purse, but they still had her credit cards. She ID'd both of them, and one of them was the nephew.

By the time we got to the preliminary the pressure was

on. Judge Fang ruled that it was okay to try the one guy, but
he wouldn't even let the victim say there was another guy.
It was like the nephew had never even been busted; nobody
had ever heard of him. And he was boasting to his street
gang how he got the case fixed.

Jim McElman, one of our uniformed guys, had a similar
experience when he busted the son of one of the state's
elected officials. The guy had a pocketful of red devils and
twenty-two joints of marijuana. At the preliminary Judge
Zeller went into closed session and dismissed the charge,
no explanation.

Of course, in a place like Beverly Hills, where most of the
people get by on who they know, not what they know, it's
as natural to use influence in court as it is to go to the bathroom. Sometimes it's like magic: You see it happening, but
you can't be sure how they do it. The only thing you're sure
about is that somebody put some clout to the judge.

That's what must have happened after we busted John
Karmann, because if it wasn't martini justice, only magic
could explain it. John was the worst of the legacies left by
his father, Harold Karmann, who was one of the classic
Hollywood moguls. The old man's other legacies included a
studio that he built from two-reel silents into one of the
majors, a lot of funny tales about his crude language, an
enormous baronial home up north of Sunset Boulevard, and
a leggy bleached blond widow, Jeanne, who thought she
was the sexiest thing to hit town since Harlow.

After old Harold was planted, Jeanne married the English
actor Horton Featheray, who was half her age; I could never
figure it out because Featheray is a fag. But to each his own.
My only interest was that some woman called me at the
station one day (she wouldn't identify herself) and told
about Jeanne and Featheray always throwing these wild
parties and sniffing coke, which John got for them.

That fitted with John's reputation. John plays at being a
stockbroker, but what he really does is spend the money his

father made. He drives a Jag and a couple of Rollses, and he
is a connoisseur of weed, which he is supposed to be buying from some guy in West LA. The cocaine I didn't know
about.

So when we got a call that John was making trouble up at
the Beverly Hills Hotel, I went along for the bust. We found
him staggering around the driveway, shouting nonsense
and disturbing the peace of the people pulling up in their
limousines to make deals in the Polo Lounge. This was no
junior high; he had had more than a small sniff of nose
candy. He was wild and violent; we had to fight him to cuff
him, to get him into the car and to get him out of the car at
the station.

Possibly LSD was involved, too, because first he was so
wild and then, after I talked with him for a while, suddenly
he turned against the dope and the guy who supplied it;
that's how LSD works on you: You love everybody one
minute, and you hate them the next.

He went wild-eyed, he rolled his head back, and he said
"Please, please, help me! Don't let me die like this! Please
go up to my place and get that stuff out of there! I'll never
touch it again!"

I said, "Where is it, John?"

"It's in my bedroom," he said. "In the chest by the window."

"Okay, I'll take care of it," I said. "But where do you get
it?"

"Oh, oh," he said, moaning. "Oh, oh, that son of a fucking bitch!"

It took a little time, but finally, he told me the guy's
name was Phil Barker and he was living in a motel on Santa
Monica Boulevard.

First I went up to the house. The maid, who had an English accent, told me that Mrs. Karmann—she still called
her that—and Mr. Featheray couldn't be disturbed. By the
whoops and giggles coming from upstairs they already were

disturbed; they had had one of their wild parties the night before, I found out, and the guests had split, but as far as those two were concerned, the party was still going.

I identified myself to the maid, and I said, "I'm here to pick up some stuff that John told me to come up and get. He says it's in his bedroom."

She gave me a kind of funny look, like she knew what I was talking about, and she said, "Where in his bedroom?"

I said, "He says it's in the chest, the window chest."

And she said, "That's probably some of the things that I took down in the cellar this morning."

"Well," I said, "let's look in the cellar and see."

It was such a big house they had an elevator, so we took the elevator to the basement, and in some cardboard boxes in a storage closet I found some plastic bags of raw grass.

I said, "Yeah, this is some of the stuff. But there's more in that chest, so would you show me the bedroom?"

And in the chest in the bedroom there was more. The total was eighteen pounds, which is a lot of grass because the stuff is very light. At that time it would have sold on the street for about $3,000.

While I was talking with the maid there in the bedroom, Featheray heard us, and he stuck his head out of a door down the hall and yelled, "If he wants any of it, tell him it's in the library behind the book rack."

Whatever it was, I wanted it, so the maid took me to the library, and here was this bookshelf that opened out on hinges, and behind it was a secret compartment. Real Hollywood. In there was a full bottle of powdered cocaine, which was what Featheray was high on and what he thought I wanted to sniff, and about a thousand pills of every illegal kind. So I confiscated all the stuff.

On my way out the front door I heard a yell, and it was Featheray, bundled up like a monk in a hooded bathrobe, sticking his head out a window on the second floor. "What's going on down there?" he said.

I said, "I came to pick up some stuff for John, Mr. Featheray."

And he said, "John? John?" Now he raised that actor's voice to calliope pitch. "Jeannie! Who the hell is John?" Jeannie came to the window and leaned out, stark naked, her tired tits hanging below the sill, and she stared down at me. I didn't think she could have seen her hand in front of her face.

"John?" she said in a voice as thin as a dollar steak. "John? That's right. That's where I was going." And she disappeared.

There was no sense in either one of them, so I just went on back to the station with my bag of goodies and booked it all in. If these people wanted to ruin their lives, it wasn't my business. My business was the suppliers, Phil Barker and John Karmann, and I decided to award myself an MD degree because John had told me the name of his psychiatrist.

I dressed properly, in a super-shaggy English sports jacket and a pair of dirty, rumpled flannel slacks. I got Zenter and Campbell to stake on the motel down on Santa Monica, and I knocked on Barker's door. Barker opened.

"Mr. Barker," I said, jerking my head a little, "my name is Dr. Arom Felzinski, and I am John Karmann's psychiatrist, and I think you and I have a problem with John's health. That concerns you, no?"

It did, so he said, "Come in, Mr. Felzinski."

And I said, "*Dr.* Felzinski, if you please, Mr. Barker." And I jerked my head harder. It's the old offended-superior routine, and it almost always works with a guy who thinks he's dealing with a professional.

He said, "I'm sorry, *Dr.* Felzinski."

And I was in.

I said, "Mr. Barker, I am very much worried about John's health. He has these flashes, he's losing control of himself, and I don't know how to treat him. I don't know exactly what he's under the influence of. But he keeps telling me all about you, he seems to almost worship you, and he tells me that everything he has, you furnished to him."

The guy was cagey. "Well," he said, "I'm not sure I know what you're talking about."

"I'm talking about my patient, John Karmann," I said. "And if we can't speak frankly, there's no point to this. John needs help, he needs it badly, and to treat him properly, I need to know exactly what drugs he has been taking; otherwise, the cure could be worse than the problem. Of course, anything you tell me will be held in strict confidence."

"Just between you, as John's doctor, and me?" he said.

I said, "Mr. Barker, I cannot violate the privacy of the physician-patient relationship."

We went around that bush half a dozen times until Barker was convinced, and finally he began to spill.

"Yeah," he said, "I supply all of John's stuff—the pills, the weed, the coke, all of it." Once he started talking, he began to brag. "John buys a lot of cocaine, and that fag Englishman who married his mother is high on it all the time. And the weed, John buys anything new, any new growth. He says he studies it. I guess he's going to be a professor of weed." The guy laughed, like it was funny.

After I got all the information I needed, I opened the door and said, "Ed, Bruce, come on in." Zenter and Campbell were staked out there on a little patio, and they stepped inside.

I introduced them to Barker and said, "Mr. Barker, as a doctor I can't hide something like this. I had no idea it was so serious. I'm obligated to let the police know what is going on. I'll work with you, and the word goes no further; but they have to be in on it and work with us to help John."

Zenter got very solemn, and he promised to try to help John, and Campbell swore the same, and for a couple of minutes the place got as sticky as a prayer meeting.

But we couldn't bust Barker; we had no evidence to connect him with the dope, only his word. When we left, I told him I'd see him again, and he promised to keep in touch. But he was really spooked. He split that same night, and I never saw him again. I heard he left the country.

We filed everything against John Karmann, and we went into Beverly Hills Municipal Court in front of Judge Arthur Hall, and funny things started to happen.

The defense attorney was Joe Bellen, a big corporation lawyer for the Karmann family and the studio, and Bellen kept asking for delays and Judge Hall kept handing them out like free balloons at the fair. Between them they dragged this case out for a whole year, and we never did get to Superior Court for a trial. The felony filings all got thrown out, one by one—the cocaine, the eighteen pounds of marijuana, the pills. Finally, the judge let John Karmann plead guilty to a misdemeanor charge of possessing one pound of weed. One pound! John got probation; he never went to jail at all.

Whether it's done with friendship, sex, political clout or just plain money, it's martini justice. It always comes with a twist.

4

Blind Justice

RUNNING A criminal court is like being President of the United States: It is strictly on-the-job training. It takes more qualifications to get hired as a pizza cook. A lawyer has to pass the bar, a teacher has to get degrees and certification, a policeman has to pass a whole set of tests and training courses, a plumber has to be licensed; but all that any clown needs to make judge is a friend in the right place.

Or $10,000. Frank Rissotti worked a case of mine when he was one of the top guys in the DA's office, and he wanted a judgeship.

"But I can't raise the money," he said.

I said, "What do you mean, the money?"

"Ten grand."

"Who gets it?" I said. "The governor?" In California it's the governor who appoints judges. Once they get appointed, they have to run for reelection now and then, but mostly they get reelected forever.

"Oh," Frank said, "he doesn't get it personally, I guess. But you got to give that much to the party. And I haven't got it."

He got it together three years later, I guess, because suddenly he was a judge. He's in Superior Court now, and he's not a bad judge; but the selection process is pretty bad. It's like getting knighted: The governor taps you on the shoulder and says, "Okay, you're it," and suddenly you're endowed with wisdom.

But nobody gets to be Solomon by appointment; you've got to understand the people you deal with. And most judges don't know criminals; they have no street knowledge. They've spent too much time backslapping and not enough in back alleys.

Every couple of years a judge ought to have to take a sabbatical, hang up his black robe and get out in the street and get his hands and his mind dirty. If he had to work with a cop kicking in doors and maybe getting shot at, or if he had to work with a parole officer and learn how criminals lie and connive and how the so-called rehabilitation programs never rehabilitate the pros, he'd think a lot differently when he stepped back up on the bench. He'd learn to distrust anybody with a rap sheet.

Like Clarence Baintree. This guy and a friend got busted outside the Beverly Hilton Hotel in a stolen car loaded with men's clothing that had just been boosted out of Robinson's department store next door.

When the arrest report crossed my desk I was about to head to downtown LA to the LAPD records bureau in the Glass House, which is what we call their headquarters at Parker Center. So among others I checked out Baintree. Sure enough, he had made a long career out of breaking the law, but he hadn't been active the last three years.

One thing didn't fit. The rap sheet showed an address in Eagle Rock, out north near Pasadena, but when he was arrested this time, Baintree gave us an address on Eighth Street near downtown LA. It was only a few blocks, so I drove by.

And I found myself staring into a vacant lot. I talked around the neighborhood, and they said the place had been a warehouse, but it had been torn down maybe ten years ago.

Back in Beverly Hills I had a talk with Tim Tanner, the bailiff in Judge Marvin Fang's court. "Tim," I said, "you got a guy coming up here on theft, Baintree."

Tim said, "Yeah, he's on the call."

I said, "Will you clue the judge that this guy has given us a phony address? It's a vacant lot." And I told him what I knew.

"Okay, I'll tell him," Tim said. "I think Haston is going to make a spiel to get him out OR."

Jerry Haston is a public defender, and this is typical of how public defenders operate. Haston wanted the court to turn Baintree loose OR, which is on his own recognizance. On pure trust, no bail required. That's like they had captured Adolf Hitler during World War II and then let him go free pending the Nuremberg trials because he had a big job and a fine reputation in Nazi Germany. The only guys you let out OR either have track records you can trust or have more to lose by splitting than by showing up for trial.

Judge Fang turned Clarence Baintree back out on the street OR. I couldn't believe it. "Tim," I said to Tanner the next day, "didn't you talk to the judge about that vacant lot?"

"Yeah, I talked to him," Tim said, "but you know how Jerry Haston cries."

"Didn't the judge even ask about it?"

Tim said, "Oh, sure, he asked. But Haston says Baintree was actually born there—it was a home forty years ago before it was a warehouse—and he says the guy is a hype and he's confused, and maybe in his terrible condition he thought he still lived there. Man, it was a real tearjerker. Took all afternoon for this courtroom to dry out."

So the guy was gone. Comes the preliminary, naturally he didn't show, and Judge Fang had to issue a bench warrant for his arrest.

About the time the judge was signing the paper, a guy with a gun walked into a dress shop on North Rodeo Drive, pulled about $300 out of the cash register, kidnapped one of the employees, Mrs. Aileen Hernandez, and split. He went to a car parked around the corner and turned Mrs. Hernandez loose there without hurting her, but if he forced her to move one inch, it's legally a kidnap.

From the descriptions I got from Mrs. Hernandez and two other witnesses, this could have been our friend Baintree. I put together a six-photo lineup of mug shots, and all three of them put the finger on him.

Now I had another reason to hunt the bastard besides Judge Fang's bench warrant, so I found the time to go out to Eagle Rock. The place was a small house, a woman answered the door, and when I explained what I wanted, she got very disturbed.

"Oh, God!" she said. "This happens all the time. That's not my husband, Clarence; it's his brother, Harold. Harold is always giving Clarence's name when he gets arrested, and you police are always coming around and hassling me about Clarence. I'm sick of it! Can't you keep your stupid records straight?"

It was a good question. I ran the whole thing again, and I found I had made a mistake. When I checked Clarence Baintree's record at the Glass House, I hadn't bothered to bring his fingerprint card back to Beverly Hills to check against ours. That hadn't seemed necessary, which only shows that you never know how little a thing is important. When I got it all sorted out, the woman was right: Her husband, Clarence, did have a record; but for three years he had been straight, and Harold Baintree was the guy I wanted.

If I hadn't made that mistake, Judge Fang probably would not have OR'd Harold Baintree, alias Clarence, and probably the dress shop robbery and kidnapping would not have happened. But my real mistake was thinking that when Judge Fang knew that Baintree had lied about his address, he would naturally assume that Baintree could not be trusted OR. I didn't realize that Judge Fang had no street knowledge.

It took me almost a year to find Baintree, he moved so fast. I tracked him through the produce market in downtown LA, through a dozen bars; for a month I was in and out of a halfway house in West LA where everybody was on dope; and finally I got a teletype: He had been busted by LAPD for another robbery, and he was in LA County Jail. I went downtown to see him.

Nobody could believe what I saw. Baintree had aged all of a sudden, the way a hype will. His brown hair had gone completely gray; he had put on fifty flabby pounds; he looked like some other guy completely. His mother wouldn't have known him.

Neither did my witnesses. One of them had disappeared in the year since the robbery, just moved away somewhere. Mrs. Hernandez and the other witness couldn't ID Baintree because he looked about as much like the guy who robbed the store as Santa Claus. Even Judge Fang couldn't recognize him as the same defendant.

All charges dismissed.

That's what happens with delays. Witnesses disappear, or defendants change, or people forget or they die, and after a while you can't make a case. Delays always work for the defense. And when the defense cons the judge into helping delay trial, the prosecution's chances of getting a conviction drop to about the level of Lake Mead if Boulder Dam breaks.

Some cases you can't make any sense out of at all. I busted a guy who snatched a purse from an old lady, Mrs. Anna Soren, at Whitworth and Almont. The guy knocked her down and dislocated her hip. She was the only witness.

When the trial came up Judge Zeller dismissed the case because Mrs. Soren was too badly hurt to leave the hospital and come to court to testify. The judge blamed the victim for her injury that was caused by the criminal! After that, the only thing that surprised me was that Judge Zeller didn't give the guy a reward.

Of course, nobody can con all of the judges all the time. But Judge Mark Binns, who sits in Superior Court in Santa Monica, would take legal advice from Attila the Hun. One of my cases that he tried ought to be printed up in law school textbooks as a classic example of blind justice.

It began with a robbery in an apartment behind the Holiday Inn, which is on Wilshire at Crescent. The people who live there, Jackson Crane and his wife, Danielle, were expecting some late guests after dinner, about midnight. Jackson told them to come in the back door because it was handy from the motel, and he made the mistake of leaving the door open for them.

The guests, who were Willis and Philla Lessinger from Palos Verdes, and a guy from Texas, Stanton Rawlings, came in the front door instead; they couldn't find the back. But before anybody could hardly say hello, a couple of guys found that open back door, accepted the invitation and joined the party. One of them, the little guy, had a gun, and they ripped off almost $10,000 in cash and jewels before they split.

They left a few things. They had stuffed some rings and watches into Philla Lessinger's purse, but they split in a hurry and forgot to take it along. And Philla got to keep one ring; she told one of the guys it had a sentimental value, and he said, "Okay, hide it then, because my partner is not as sentimental as I am."

Two weeks later LAPD busted Beardsley Cheney, Jr., and Hal Fulliam for committing two robberies in twelve minutes, one where they ripped off a lady in a telephone booth behind the Holiday Inn in Beverly Hills and the other where they robbed a store just over the LA line on La Cienega. The storeowner phoned a quick alarm, and a black and white unit spotted them and busted them with the loot just three blocks away.

Both those jobs belonged to LAPD because they made the bust, but the descriptions of the two guys sounded like the guys I wanted for the Crane job. So did the MO: They hit targets of opportunity, no planning at all, same area.

I sat Jackson and Danielle Crane down, and I ran more than 200 photographs by them. They both picked out Cheney and Fulliam, positive IDs.

Next, I took them to Superior Court in downtown LA, where Cheney and Fulliam were making an appearance on the LAPD charges.

"Look around," I said, "and see if you recognize anybody."

They looked around, and right away they fingered Cheney and Fulliam, sitting in the audience in the back. This is a perfect lineup, twenty or thirty people of all kinds, and nobody could claim we rigged it. So when the two guys walked out of the courtroom, we busted them right there in the courthouse corridor.

And now the hassle began.

Cheney's father, Beardsley Cheney, Sr., was a mailman, and he dropped into the Cranes' boutique on Rodeo Drive and laid on this bit about how his son was a fine boy and it would be terrible for him to be convicted of a crime when he made just one little mistake. And underneath all this malarkey was a hint of something happening to Jackson and Danielle if they testified against Beardsley, Jr.

Jackson called me right away; he was worried, and Danielle was scared half to death. So I drove down to the Terminal Annex Post Office for a talk with Beardsley's old man.

"Yeah," he said, "I went out and discussed the case with them. Mr. Wright told me to."

I couldn't believe it, even of Connor Wright, who was Beardsley's attorney. Wright is a venal bastard who got kicked off the DA's staff for something that nobody will even talk about, but it takes stupidity, as well as crookedness, to encourage a defendant's father to go out and threaten prosecution witnesses.

"Did he tell you to threaten them?" I said.

"He told me I could talk to them any way I wanted to," said Beardsley, Sr.

He didn't know any better, so all I said was, "Okay, Mr. Cheney, now you listen. If I get one more word of you going out and hassling my victims, just one more word, I'm going to come back down here and take you into custody."

Then I got Connor Wright on the phone and I told him what had happened.

"Mr. Franklin," he said in a voice like cyclamates, "there must be some mistake."

"Yeah," I said, "and it's yours. So help me God, if I get one more kickback out of this, *you* are going to need a defense attorney because I'm going to come down to your office and bust you for impeding justice."

Even that didn't stop the hassling. Lawyers like Connor Wright stay awake nights thinking up ways to hassle the victims of their clients, mainly because the judges will let them get away with it and it makes a lot of witnesses back off.

The preliminary before Judge Armand Zeller in Beverly Hills Municipal Court should have taken only one day, but it took two because Connor Wright didn't even show until four o'clock in the afternoon. The judge had people phoning all over town for him all day, but when Wright finally strolled into the court, Zeller just slapped him on the wrist and ordered everybody back the next day.

While I was in the courtroom with the DA listening to other cases and waiting for Connor Wright to do Judge Zeller the favor of showing up, all the witnesses in our case were ordered to stay out in the corridor except when they were called in to testify. The judicial theory is this keeps them honest. It's like using a chastity belt to gag a whore: It may keep her quiet, but it won't keep her out of business. The thieves have already coordinated their lies.

But I didn't know about what was happening outside until I strolled out during a recess and found all my prosecution witnesses with sweaty palms.

"Can't you put a stop to this?" Willis Lessinger said. He was all excited and red in the face.

I said, "To what?"

"These people are deliberately bothering us," he said, and he pointed to a bunch of defense witnesses standing a little way off, all of them wearing their crocheted caps and their high heels, all looking over at us.

Jackson Crane said, "The girls are getting upset, and I sure don't like it either."

I said, "What are they doing?"

"They keep walking by where we're sitting," Philla Lessinger said, "and they keep coming closer and closer, when there's plenty of room, so we have to draw our feet back. And they keep saying things."

"Saying what?"

"It's a threatening attitude," Willis said. "They go by, and they talk to each other, but it's for our benefit, and they're saying what liars we are and how could we do this to their innocent friends, and they wouldn't want to be us if their friends are convicted, things like that."

"Okay," I said, "I'll take care of it."

I went over to those guys, and I said, "Look, you scum, you leave those witnesses alone. Stop hassling them. Don't talk to them, don't even talk so they can hear you, and don't go close to them."

"Hey, man," one of them said, "this is a free country. You can't order us around like that."

And I said, "I just did, you motherfucker! Try any of that stuff once more, and I'll bust the whole bunch of you right here, and you'll find out how free this country is."

From then on all the hassling was official; it came from the judges and the defense lawyers. Judge Zeller and Connor Wright got the first crack at Philla Lessinger when she testified how the bandits dumped stuff in her purse and then split so fast they forgot to take it along.

"Is that the same purse you're carrying now?" Connor Wright said.

It happened to be, and Wright asked the court to attach the purse as evidence, and Judge Zeller said okay. This was nothing but harassment because it could have been any purse—it wouldn't have made any difference in the trial—but they took it anyway. They dumped everything out, and Philla had to take her things home in a paper sack.

By the time we went to trial before Judge Mark Binns in Superior Court in Santa Monica, Beardsley Cheney, Jr., had got himself another lawyer, Eugene Cermak. At least he got to court on time. Aside from that, the only difference between Connor Wright and Eugene Cermak is that Wright tears honest people apart on the witness stand and then boasts about it, while Cermak asks forgiveness for his sins afterward. But that doesn't stop him from committing them.

The judge's behind still hadn't got the bench warm when Cermak was objecting to any mention of the other two robberies Cheney and Fulliam got busted for in LA two weeks after the Crane job. This is SOP in American criminal trials; any information that the defendant has ever done anything more antisocial than hit a flat note in choir practice is a violation of his constitutional right to rip people off. The judge agreed; one word about this, he said, and he would declare a mistrial.

The judge went so far in suppressing any bad news about the defendants that he wouldn't even allow me to tell the jury that they had been arrested in a courtroom. All I could say is that it happened at 212 West Temple Street in downtown LA, which is the Criminal Court Building.

This knocked out our case on MO, because the jury was not to know that these two sons of bitches make a habit of robbing people.

Next, Judge Binns started knocking out our witnesses. We had already decided it was not worth bringing Stanton Rawlings back from Texas to testify, because they made him lie facedown on a sofa and he didn't see much of anything that happened. Now we lost Danielle Crane, and we lost Philla Lessinger as far as identifying Cheney and Fulliam was concerned.

Philla could testify about what happened, the judge said, but she wasn't allowed to ID the guys because the first time she ID'd them it was out of a lineup of six mug shots we showed her. That wasn't enough, Judge Binns ruled. It might have influenced her judgment; it was like embezzling the evidence.

So John Peruzza, the deputy DA, tried to teach the judge a little law. He had to talk carefully because Mark Binns has an ego that bruises easily; he can go from sweetness to a shark smile to insane rage in two seconds. Philla Lessinger said it was "like pulling window shades up and down."

"Your Honor," John said, "I believe the law, as it stands now by the Supreme Court, is that identification shall not be suppressed by the court if the people can demonstrate that the identification in no way had anything to do with the photographs. And her testimony, uncontradicted, on the stand at the time of the preliminary was that when she saw them in court it was very clear in her mind that these were the two people."

Judge Binns, like a lot of judges, would rather not hear about the Supreme Court unless its ruling favors the defendant. "You're going to have a problem," he told John, "and the problem will be that she must not in the presence of the jury indicate that either of the two defendants did it." And he put on that shark smile.

It was almost like we had to try to convict these two guys

of a crime that nobody committed. Of course, we had started out with solid IDs. Both Jackson and Danielle Crane ID'd Cheney and Fulliam during our investigation, first out of more than 200 photos and then in person in the downtown courtroom. We cut the photo lineup to half a dozen for Philla because running 200 mug shots by her was a waste of time; we already knew who had done the job. But Judge Binns' idea of proper police conduct is for us to keep spinning our wheels.

And we couldn't get Danielle Crane at all. Since the preliminary she had split with Jackson and gone back home to Dallas, and she was scared to come back and face those two bandits in the courtroom. So she got a psychiatrist in Dallas to say she was in no condition to come to LA.

This hurt because we had figured Danielle for our star witness; one $4,500 diamond ring they took from her was almost half the loot, plus which Fulliam had put his gun to her head when he marched her into the bedroom to get the jewelry.

But there was no use dragging her to LA; a reluctant witness won't help a case. So we made arrangements for her to give a deposition to a judge in Dallas.

Eugene Cermak wanted none of that. The mental picture of Fulliam putting his gun to a woman's head might make the jury realize that a crime was committed. So Cermak objected, and Judge Binns called the lawyers up to the bench.

"Have you talked to this psychiatrist?" he said to John Peruzza.

John said, "Yes, Your Honor. On the telephone."

"Well, what do you think?"

"I think," John said, "that the psychiatrist needs a psychiatrist. But he leaves us no alternative except the deposition."

"Well," said Judge Binns, "I am not going to let some Texas judge tell me how to run my court. The deposition will not be admitted." And he gave John the shark smile again.

All we could use of Danielle was her testimony at the preliminary in Beverly Hills, which wasn't enough to help. The only reason for a preliminary is to establish that the defendants ought to be held for trial; you don't try to prove the case until you get to the actual trial. So we lost our star witness, and Philla's ID of the bandits, and every witness you lose weakens your case.

None of this made any sense to Philla Lessinger; she had never even been inside a courtroom before. "This judge is treating us like criminals," she said.

"Yeah," I said, "in Judge Binns' court everybody is treated like a criminal unless he is one."

That includes cops. I had a back injury which later came down to spinal surgery, and the morning of the day I was scheduled to testify, which was a Friday, I had a spinal tap at St. John's Hospital in Santa Monica. It was so painful I couldn't even sit down, but Judge Binns wouldn't put me over to Monday. The only concession he made was he let me testify standing up. If any judge ever treated a defendant that way, the Supreme Court would turn the guy loose and throw the judge in jail.

When a defendant is guilty as hell, his lawyer doesn't fight the state's case; he fights the state's witnesses. Cermak picked on Philla Lessinger until she was almost in tears on the witness stand. He tried to make her admit that she was too tired to know what was going on the night of the robbery, she was confused about Danielle Crane's height, her eyesight was so bad she couldn't have seen much of anything anyway, and she was maybe drunk on cocktails she had had at dinner.

The facts are she slept late that morning and never felt tired all day; she had never seen Danielle Crane until about a minute before the robbery, and the only other time was at the preliminary; she does wear glasses, but only for reading; and she had one glass of wine with dinner at the Great American Food and Beverage Company in Santa Monica, a restaurant where they don't serve hard liquor. She testified to all this.

But a shyster like Cermak made his points with his own questions, not with her answers. He couldn't care less what she said. All he wanted was for the jury to get a general impression that the witness was incompetent.

Later, out in the corridor, Cermak came up all apologies to Philla, and he told her what a pleasure it was to deal with such an honest witness. And he talked a lot about his wife and two daughters, laying on the idea that he is a loving family man, which maybe he is.

"I hope this wasn't too unpleasant for you, Mrs. Lessinger," he said. "You know, I'm only doing my job."

She let him have it. "Well," she said, "I only hope it's not your wife and two daughters that somebody holds a gun at their temple next time." And she walked away from him.

It didn't bother Cermak; he's just an act anyway. Part of the act is destroy the credibility of the prosecution's witnesses, and the other part is make the defendant look like the chairman of the board. Cheney and Fulliam walked into that courtroom like they owned it; they'd trimmed their hair, and Fulliam had shaved off his straggly mustache, and they were wearing $350 suits they bought with their stolen money.

That's the only way a judge ever sees a criminal: showered and shaved and looking like a gentleman. Professional criminals are always on their best behavior in court; they don't shout or throw things around or have to be tied and gagged—that's for radicals who want to wreck the system. The criminal wouldn't change anything about the system— it's too good to him. He just wants to cheat it.

Everything that happened up to now was petty stuff compared to what happened when Cermak started putting on

Cheney's defense. Cermak should get the Pulitzer Prize for fiction.

The way the story went, Beardsley Cheney, Jr., was not out robbing people that night; he was running around town with a bunch of friends, watching television and playing bid whist and dominoes, from ten o'clock at night until about two in the morning, which conveniently covered the midnight robbery. And Cermak had the witnesses to prove it.

Beardsley and one guy remembered seeing Chad Everett on *Medical Center* a little after ten o'clock. They wandered around, picked up some other guys; they all watched the eleven o'clock news at Beardsley's place; then a little before midnight they dropped in on another guy, William Lane, who had his girlfriend over, and they watched Johnny Carson on the *Tonight* show.

This happened about nine months ago by the time we heard it in court, but all five witnesses remembered it well. Beardsley even remembered the funny turban Johnny Carson wore in one skit. It was an unbreakable alibi.

Except that we put on a guy from CBS, Bill Noethens, who brought in the station log of KNXT, which is the CBS station in Los Angeles, and CBS proved for us that *Medical Center* wasn't on the air that night. It was preempted by a *CBS Reports* special on Watergate.

And except that we put on NBC's unit manager of the *Tonight* show, Terri Collum, and she said the show did not begin at its usual time, eleven thirty; it was delayed half an hour by an NBC special on Watergate. On top of which, Johnny Carson was off sick that night and Joey Bishop substituted for him.

There was no way those people could have seen Chad Everett on *Medical Center* that night, and there was no way they could have watched the *Tonight* show before midnight, and there was no way they could have seen Johnny Carson, funny turban or bare-bottom naked.

The best thing to come out of Watergate was that what

was scheduled on TV that night was not what happened. A couple of defense witnesses even admitted under cross-examination that just two weeks before the trial they had looked up that night's TV programs on microfilm of an old *TV Guide* in the Inglewood library. Eugene Cermak put them up to it, but that didn't come out; the lawyer never gets involved.

Okay, add it all up, and there was no way the prosecution could lose this case. We had the father of one defendant threatening witnesses, which is obstructing justice. We had a defense attorney fabricating lies for his witnesses, which is subornation of perjury and obstructing justice. We had five defense witnesses lying on the stand, which is perjury. And all seven of these people were guilty of contempt of court.

So what did Judge Mark Binns do? Nothing. Nothing at all. He issued no contempt citations; he made no request to the DA to file charges; he didn't even warn the jury that the testimony on the record proved that either the defense witnesses or the network people committed perjury, take your choice. He just sat there on his august ass and let a bunch of criminals and their dishonest lawyer pervert his court.

And we got a hung jury.

The jury never knew the truth. Juries never do because judges won't let them know the truth. Every time I have to stand up there and put my hand on the Bible and swear to tell the truth, the whole truth and nothing but the truth, so help me God, I ask God to forgive me because it's all a lie. The judge won't let me tell the truth.

The jury system made sense, a long time ago, when you had to know all the parties to the case and all the gossip to be qualified to serve on the jury; all anybody needed to be fair was common sense. Now the judge disqualifies anybody who knows the time of day; he doesn't trust ordinary people, and he thinks all jurors are stupid. If it's a big case and the state can afford it, he isolates the jury, like germs in a test tube; if he could, he'd impanel a jury from another planet.

This change didn't happen all at once, but when it did, when the judiciary became some kind of self-anointed priesthood, truth stopped being the object of the legal process. Now it's all tricks with the law, and don't annoy the defendant. If the prosecution lies, the judge will throw somebody in jail. But if the defense lies, that's okay; that's just "putting on the case." You won't find that in the lawbooks, but that's the way the system is run.

John Peruzza nearly blew an artery. "A new trial?" he said to me. "Damn! The DA is already on my back about this one, we spent so much of the people's money."

Which is another thing that never shows in the court records and is not discussed in the law books. Crimeonomics. When you have a case like this, which makes no big news, the DA's office gets nervous about the budget. For a Charles Manson trial or a Patty Hearst trial you can get anything you need, but those are one in a million. Most people never hear of most criminal cases, the other 999,999 little cases which are the real reason we have more major crimes year after year. As far as the judge is concerned, trials are run in some kind of never-never land where money barely gets mentioned, but the first rule of crimeonomics is, if you don't get the publicity, you don't get the money to prosecute.

Peruzza must have done one hell of a sales job downtown because we got a new trial.

And we got more hassles and delays. The defense got sixteen postponements in the two trials; the prosecution got zero; the victims and the witnesses got zero. It's a fair measure of how the judge leans; nobody has problems but the defense.

Willis Lessinger's problem was survival. Willis was a manufacturer's representative in furniture, and twice a year there is a big LA furniture and gift show where he sets up displays and takes orders and buyers come in from stores all over the country. This is where he makes his living; there was no way he could miss it. And for a while the second trial was supposed to start during the furniture and gift show.

So Willis called up John Peruzza to see if he could get a postponement, and John said, "Sorry, Willis, but there is nothing we can do. Nobody listens to us. You'll have to call the judge."

Willis called Judge Binns and laid the problem on him, and the judge said, "That's no excuse." The Lessingers could go on welfare, it was no concern of his; the trial was going to start when the defense wanted it.

Willis started to get mad, and he said, "I don't like the decision you're giving me. I'm going to go over your head. Who's in charge of you?"

That must have sent the judge right up the wall. "Nobody is in charge of me," he said. "I am the judge. If you want to, you can go to church and ask God, but I'm not granting your postponement."

All John Peruzza could give Willis was sympathy. "Yeah," John said, "that's the way it goes. Some people think those three little steps up to the bench put them closer to God. And some of them think it makes them God."

Lucky for Willis, the defense asked for another delay and got it, and the trial started two days after his furniture show ended.

This time around we completely lost both our women. The Lessingers were mad and bitter by now, Philla saw no point in testifying if she couldn't ID the bandits, and Willis said, "I won't have her subjected to this idiocy again." Peruzza had to go along with that.

And Judge Binns threw out Danielle Crane's testimony from the preliminary hearing, which he allowed at the first trial. That's judicial consistency.

Everything else was pretty much the same routine, except the defense alibi was all changed; there was no mention of *Medical Center* or Johnny Carson. Judge Binns sat up there and let them get away with it, like he had never heard a different story from the same mouths. And the jurors were all new and didn't know the truth; they had no way of knowing that this was more perjury.

They acquitted Cheney and Fulliam.

"Oh, my God!" one of them said when we told her afterward about the other two robberies. "If we had known, we'd have convicted them!"

Another one told me, "The attitude of the judge caused me to vote for acquittal. He seemed to convey a feeling that these people were not guilty, and I felt that he was in a position to know."

"I can't believe it!" Philla Lessinger said. "What happened?"

John said, "The judge is what happened. He is an erratic, petulant judge who did his best to keep out the people's evidence. We have too many judges like him, and they are the reason the system isn't protecting society. They are the reason the crime rate is going up."

"Well," she said, "I'll tell you one thing; I won't be treated like a criminal again when I'm not. Not after what we went through. I'll never identify anybody again."

John said, "What if you're a victim again?"

And she said, "I'll get myself off the hook. I won't know anything. I'm just a ball of hate now, and so is Willis, and we didn't go into it with that attitude at all. No wonder people are losing confidence in the system; it doesn't deserve any!"

That's how it happens all the time. Justice is blind because the judge is blind to the con games lawyers and criminals play. And when it's all over, he goes back into that ivory tower he calls his chambers, he takes off his robe and hangs it up, he pats himself on the back for being such a great servant of the people, and he splits out the back door.

In the courtroom he leaves the police and the DA to try to explain what happened to the angry victims and the frustrated witnesses.

And nobody gives a damn, until it happens to them.

5

The Red Velvet Snare

THERE IS no place easier to rip off office buildings than Beverly Hills. In most of the buildings along Wilshire Boulevard and Olympic Boulevard they leave the main entrance open until late at night because people are working late and somebody is always forgetting his key. All you have to do is walk in, get up to one of the floors, jimmy a lock and take whatever you want. Every thief I know tells me Beverly Hills is an easy mark.

Electric office machines, like typewriters, calculators, photocopiers, are worth about $800 apiece. The thief sticks one in the trunk of his car, and he drives into a filling station—just about any filling station, anywhere.

"Hey," he says, "I'm closing out a service station myself, and I got an extra calculator I'll sell you. What'll you give me for it?"

The guy will give him two or three hundred, no questions asked. He knows it's stolen, but he doesn't care. The price is right, and a filling station owner can always use a calculator.

We always have petty little operations like that going on. Everybody does. But in 1970, 1971 something else began to happen. Somebody got organized.

They began to go into a building and rip off a whole floor at a time. One night they hit 8447 Wilshire and cleaned out *four* floors, and that became the pattern. They'd take everything in a building, thirty to fifty machines on a single job. They were hitting all over LA and up to Santa Barbara and down in Orange County, but they favored Beverly Hills because of the easy pickings. It was every goddamned night, and it was the biggest continuing commercial burglary operation in the entire history of crime. The take was running higher than $6,000,000 a year!

It was my problem because by now I was a detective in charge of major crimes—burglary, robbery, homicide. And those guys were so slick I couldn't lay a finger on them. Every morning we'd find a building cleaned out, every lock busted, and not a fingerprint. I couldn't even get a clue to where they were fencing the stuff; it was the greatest disappearing act since Judge Crater.

The people getting ripped off were complaining to the mayor and the City Council, and the politicians were jumping on Chief Cork, and Cork was telling me that we were looking Little League and wondering why I couldn't get something going, and I couldn't even go home and kick my dog because he's bigger than I am.

Finally, somebody made a little mistake. A guy named Harry Andrews made the mistake of trying to drive his girlfriend home after taking on too much juice. He pulled out of a place called the Red Velvet Snare, on Sunset Boulevard in Hollywood, weaving like a rugmaker, and he got no more than a block before LAPD pulled him over. Harry couldn't pass a balloon test with Binaca.

Now a couple of funny things showed up. Somebody had made another mistake and left an IBM calculator in the trunk of the car. It was routine for me to learn about it, I ran it, and it had been stolen in one of our big Beverly Hills ripoffs. That got me going.

The other funny thing was that we couldn't make the car.

It didn't belong to Harry, and the guy it was registered to was a straight citizen who had sold it for cash about six months back. He didn't know the buyer. It was nobody's car, which is impossible.

Okay, now I wanted to talk to Harry Andrews. Harry was working in a Safeway store as a meat cutter, which is a laugh. He had done time in Chino prison, and he had learned to cut meat there. The federal government has a program where they teach a con a trade, and when the guy gets out, anybody who hires him has to pay only half his salary. The government, which is you and I, pays the rest.

But Harry's caper with the pork chops was only to keep his parole officer off his back. Harry's real business was burglary. He was a hillside jewelry thief; he got invited to a lot of parties in those houses up in the Hollywood Hills, and later he went back and ripped them off.

He belonged to LA on the 502, so I went over to Safeway and busted him out from behind the meat counter for receiving the stolen IBM calculator, which gave me an excuse to strike up a conversation.

"Whose car is it, Harry?"

"Hell, I don't know."

"What do you mean, you don't know? Unless you stole it."

"No, no, I didn't steal it! I borrowed it."

"Okay, say you borrowed it. Who'd you borrow it from?"

"Like I told you, Franklin, I was drunk, I don't remember the guy."

"Sure, just like you don't remember your sainted mother. Harry, you're full of shit!"

"Jesus! A guy gets a little drunk, and you want to make a federal case out of it!"

"Well, where did the IBM thing come from?"

"How the hell would I know?"

"How the hell wouldn't you know? It was in your car."

"It's *not* my car!"

"Then whose is it?"

"If I could remember, I'd tell you. For all the trouble that bastard and his car got me into, I'd *like* to see you bust him."

"Okay, then you're ready to cooperate?"

"Sure, anything."

"Whose car is it?"

"Goddammit, Franklin, how many times I got to tell you I don't know?"

"I'll tell you how many times, Harry. As many times as it takes until you tell me what you *do* know, you son of a goddamned bitch! I got all the time in the world, and you're not going *anywhere* until you start making conversation instead of crap."

We went around and around this way for the better part of seventy-two hours. That little interrogation room, which is on the second floor of the station in Beverly Hills, in the City Hall building, is only about twice as big as a closet in the first place. And when a guy has gone through seventy-two hours of questions and lies, with damned little sleep and nothing to look at except the wall and my ugly face, that room gets smaller and smaller.

Finally, I figured Harry was beginning to feel the walls close in. I stood up and stuck my head out the door and yelled for the jailer to come get him. "Okay, Harry," I said, like it was all over. "That's it."

He looked surprised. "You're going to let me go?"

"Let you go?" I said. "Hell, no, I'm not going to let you go! You're on parole, you son of a bitch, and I'm going to send you back to state prison. I'm going to make you on *all* these big commercial rip-offs. I'm going to clear the books with you, Harry. By the time they let you out again the only hillside place you'll be headed for is Forest Lawn."

We put him back in the lockup, and pretty soon he wanted to see me again.

"Okay," he said. "Okay. What happens if I tell you something?"

I said, "I can't do anything about the 502. But I can kill the receiving charge. I can talk to your parole officer. I can keep you on the street."

He said, "What if you're conning me?"

"You got no choice," I told him.

He decided to do business with me. "The car is Ben Colt's," he said.

I ran that name through my head and drew a blank. "Who's Ben Colt?"

Harry said, "It'll blow your mind. He's the leader. If he didn't steal that IBM calculator they found in the trunk, somebody else in the gang did. It's the biggest organized gang I ever came across, maybe forty guys, and Ben Colt is the leader."

"Where do I find Colt?"

Harry said, "You know where the Red Velvet Snare is? That's where he hangs out. They all do, the whole gang. It's headquarters. You can find Colt there any afternoon, any evening, unless he's out on a job."

Now I debated. I could have gone right then and busted Colt for receiving the calculator. But I knew the district attorney wouldn't file it for me. He would say, "The calculator was recovered in Colt's car, but in the arrest of another man. Colt was a block away in the Red Velvet Snare; maybe he knew nothing about it. The courts will throw it out." He would use the same kind of reasoning on the receiving charge against Harry Andrews, too, but Harry didn't know that. The DA would say, "Andrews had borrowed the car from Colt. We can't prove that he even knew the calculator existed." I had the physical evidence, but I didn't have a case.

I went to Wayne Rutherford. "Wayne," I said, "we got a chance to really bust this whole thing. I got a plan."

"What is it?"

"I'll be the snitch."

Wayne said, "You? How the hell can you be the snitch?"

I said, "I'll work from inside. I'll get Harry to get me in the gang."

Wayne said, "You're crazy! They'll kill you!"

"Look," I said, "this is the only break we've had, but we can't go anywhere with it. We got to find out who the others are besides Colt, and we've got to bust them on the job."

"I don't like it," Wayne said.

"How else are we going to do it?"

He couldn't answer that. Nobody could. So we set it up. I got myself fitted out with a new name, Frank Franko, and the department's ID technician, Sam Bottleman, took mug shots like I had been arrested. And I had to dress the part.

Harry Andrews said, "Goddammit, don't come down there dressed like a construction worker. Every cop who tries to get in with a gang, they wear a construction jacket, they wear engineer boots, they might even carry a hard hat in the car. Any time a guy walks in looking like a construction worker, we give him a second look."

Harry said the guys dressed kind of stylish casual, so I wore a pair of black flared trousers, washables, and a black belt with a shiny silver buckle and a black tank top.

And that same afternoon I walked into the Red Velvet Snare and ordered a drink. It is a nice little layout, with a cocktail lounge with a fireplace and tables and chairs on the right as you go in and a long bar on the left. Beyond the bar is a serving place for food, where they had hors d'oeuvres out most of the time, and there is a jukebox and a little dance floor back there.

The only people in the place were three guys sitting at the bar in the back and a bartender. I took a barstool up front. It looked like they were drinking beer, so that's what I drank.

In a few minutes Harry Andrews walked in, just the way

we had arranged it. He walked right past me and joined the guys in the back. LA has the world's darkest bars, and the Red Velvet Snare is no exception, so the way it worked was like Harry was a little blinded when he first walked in.

He had a drink, and after a little while he looked over at me and yelled, "Hey, Frank!" He ran over and grabbed me. "When the hell did you get out?" And pretty soon he said, "Come on over here and meet my friends," and he introduced me as a buddy he had met in Chino.

The guys were Ben Colt, and Robin Black, who was usually called Black Rob, and Vance Menard. The bartender, Curt, was also the owner of the place. Later in the afternoon some more guys drifted in, and I met some of them. But nobody in the place was the kind of guy you would take for a criminal. There was all kinds of casual talk, and for a week nothing was said about any criminal activity, except that one bit about me just getting out of Chino. I would drop in every afternoon and evening, and it was always pretty much the same bunch of guys, only a few in the afternoon but a big crowd in the evening.

Beginning about happy hour, the girls would start to stroll in, each one sexier than the next in miniskirts or hot pants or braless, whatever advertised the best they had to offer. A couple of them worked as secretaries in big law firms, one on Hollywood Boulevard and the other down on Wilshire in the Miracle Mile; after working with lawyers all day, they came into the Red Velvet Snare and played with these thieves at night. Sometimes it's hard to tell the difference.

At night that little dance floor always got a workout, and there was a lot of fooling around, but sex wasn't the big attraction. Smart thieves are too busy calculating angles to pay all that much attention to curves. For the girls it was mostly a social thing; hanging around the Red Velvet Snare was a lot more interesting than going home to a lonely apartment and reading *Cosmopolitan*. If an occasional mattress massage was involved, well, that was enjoyable, too. Besides, everything was free for the girls because all those guys were big spenders. It was an ego thing with them, and it wasn't their money; it was stolen money. It was nothing for Black Rob to come in and throw a $100 bill on the bar and say, "Drink up, eat up, everybody! It's on the house!"

I didn't push myself on anybody because those people don't like to be pushed at any time. I'd just go in and have a couple of drinks, mind my own business and leave. But after about a week we decided to encourage some progress.

I stayed away one afternoon, and Bruce Campbell and Roger Bedford dropped in. They are Beverly Hills detectives, and Bruce, who is my partner, is maybe the best damned detective in the world except for one thing: He *looks* like a cop. He keeps his hair trimmed short enough to satisfy a Marine Corps drill instructor, he dresses the part in regulation slacks and sports jacket, and he has the build of a bulldozer. Bruce and I drive down into the jungle, and we think we're really undercover, and some little kid six years old will come up to Bruce and say, "Hey, Mr. Policeman, who you looking for today?"

But for this visit to the Red Velvet Snare, a guy with "cop" written all over him is perfect casting. Bruce and Roger came in with the fake mug shots of me that Sam Bottleman had taken. They showed them around, and the story was that they had sent me up years ago and now I was out and they had lost my trail, and it was nothing serious, you understand, but they wanted to talk to this son of a bitch Franko.

Naturally, nobody had ever seen me.

That same evening I was sitting at the bar and Ben Colt came over. "Hey, Franko," he said, "come on, I'll buy you a drink."

He took me over to a table by the fireplace, where we were alone, and he bought a couple of drinks. "You know," he said, "I know how it is when you just get out. If there's anything I can do to help you get on your feet, just speak up."

I said, "Thanks, Colt. I've been thinking about what to do."

"Well, we got a thing going here," he said. "I'm in the office machine business."

I said, "Yeah? What do you mean, office machines?"

And he said, "You know, calculators, copy machines, that kind of stuff. IBM mostly. Nothing but electric; I don't touch manual."

"You give me an idea," I said. "I decided already that I was in the wrong business. I went up as a hillside jewelry thief, but I'm not going back into that. More and more our guys are getting their heads blown off breaking into a house where some nut is sleeping with a gun under his pillow."

"Yeah," he said, "people are really getting crazy."

Colt thought that I was into hijacking now, because that was what Harry Andrews was laying out about me, so I said, "I'm doing other stuff now, but I'd like to try something new."

"Well," he said, "give it a thought and let me know."

"Okay."

The conversation was over, but he sat there and kept looking at me. "You're carrying a gun," he said.

I was carrying a personal gun, a snub-nose .38 with hollow-nose bullets, which is my friend in trouble. With that ammunition it's as good as a shotgun in close quarters. I hadn't shown the gun to anybody in the Red Velvet Snare, but I had let it be noticed by the bulge.

"Yeah," I said, "I might have a problem."

Colt said, "I know. A couple of cops were in here this afternoon looking for you. From Beverly Hills."

I said, "Those sons of bitches! They won't leave a guy alone!"

"Okay," he said. "I understand the problem."

I said, "I don't mean to cause trouble."

"There's only a couple of the guys besides me that carry guns in here," he said. "I don't like it in here, unless there's a reason. Krawczyk carries one. And Black Rob always carries a can of Mace. You got a reason, so that's okay. Just so I know about it."

A couple of nights later I hadn't said anything yet. I was letting Colt push it if he wanted to. He bought another drink, and he said, "We're going on a job tonight. Want to come along?"

He wanted me in because if I wasn't in, it bothered him; he couldn't be sure of me. So suddenly I got an engraved invitation.

"Sure," I said, "if I won't get in the way. I'd like to see how you do it."

It was a real eye-opener. Those guys had an assembly line operation that made the Chevy assembly plant in Van Nuys look like a primitive handicraft shop. The place was on Sunset Boulevard in Hollywood, a small office building with a subterranean garage that had a padlocked accordion-steel gate. Colt drove—he always drove when he went along on a job—and the other guys were Black Rob, Vance Menard and Skow Pucinski. The car was an unmarked van.

Colt pulled right up in front of the garage gate about three in the morning, Black Rob jumped out and cut the padlock with a fireman's bolt cutter, and we drove inside as big as you please. They closed the gate and locked it up again with a padlock they had brought along, so if anybody came around, the place would look secure. All this took maybe a minute.

Inside, Black Rob turned out to be a virtuoso of the vise grips, those pliers that lock onto anything and won't let go until you want them to. Skow supplied them; but it was Black Rob who used them, and it didn't take him ten minutes to strip every lock in the building. There is a trick to stripping a lock: You have to clamp those grips on and twist just so, or you break the bolt off wrong and it falls into the locked position. Then you've got to kick the door to get in. Black Rob just went down each hallway, busting every lock so fast you could hardly follow him, and he never made one mistake. That's all he did, bust the locks; the other guys loaded the stuff into the van.

Later I learned that they even had training sessions. Colt and Black Rob decided one afternoon to send some of the guys to school, and they picked an insurance building in Glendale, on San Fernando Road just three blocks from the Glendale police station.

"Make it a Sunday school," Colt said. "Nobody will be around on Sunday morning."

I tipped the Glendale PD, and I told them, "Set on it if you want to, but don't move in on them unless they take something. I just want to be posted."

Glendale staked on the building, and Skow and Black Rob took half a dozen of the guys in there, and they stripped every lock in the place. After about an hour they walked out without taking anything, so nobody touched them. But they were watched all the time.

Skow was very particular about getting the vise grips back after a job. He issued them like an army quartermaster, and he would get upset as hell if somebody lost a pair and he didn't get them back. They all wore gloves, which prevented fingerprints, but the bite marks that vise grips make on a lock can identify the tool. Now I found out why we had never been able to find a pair of vise grips that matched the marks on any job in Beverly Hills.

"Nobody is going to make my grips," Skow told me. "I just drive out to the end of the pier in Santa Monica and throw them into the ocean. If anybody ever bothers to dredge them up, they'll be too corroded to ID."

So this night these guys went through that building on Sunset like a laxative overdose. They got about twenty machines, about $16,000 worth. I just stood around and watched and learned, feeling a little guilty about letting it happen, but I had to get into the gang to bust them. Now I was in.

We left the place all locked up tidy, and Colt drove around for a while to make sure we weren't being tailed. Then he headed south on Crenshaw, and we wound up at the little airport in Inglewood, where it was mostly private and business planes—general aviation. He pulled right through the big open doors into a hangar marked CJS.

"Come on, Franko," Colt said. "I told you we got something going."

We went into an office, and I met Bill Carpenter, the owner. CJS stood for Carpenter Jet Service. This guy had that lean, beat-up look of an old war pilot, with blue eyes like ice water and weather lines around them starting to sag a little. In maybe fifty years he had lived a lot.

He stuck his head out the door and yelled, and a couple of mechanics, or whatever, came running from somewhere, and the efficiency was amazing. It wasn't half an hour before they had that load of hot machines all crated and stenciled with signs like THIS END UP and EXPORT ONLY and FRAGILE—DELICATE INSTRUMENT. They loaded them into an executive-type jet parked in the hangar and wheeled it outside.

There was a girl I hadn't noticed at first, which means I really was impressed. She was typing forms, putting in numbers which Carpenter and the mechanics kept yelling at her.

All of a sudden Bill Carpenter went outside and got in that goddamned airplane with one of the mechanics, and they took off.

My jaw must have been hanging loose because Ben Colt grinned at me and said, "Hawaii. We got a big warehouse there. We sell almost full retail in Hong Kong, Singapore, Manila, you name it. Sometimes we unload them in Mexico City. Wherever it goes, we don't fence it. Franko, we got a full service organization."

Now I knew why we had never been able to find the stuff. Colt was bragging, the way all thieves will when they think it's safe, and I didn't want to discourage him. So all I said was, "Jesus Christ!"

Colt said, "Carpenter handles all my transportation. I use him all the time to fly grass to Boston. He's safer than Brink's."

"Boston?" I said.

"It's the number one market right now," Colt said. "Detroit's pretty good too. I pay ninety a kilo here, maybe only ten if I bring it in myself. In Boston they're paying one fifty, one sixty."

This was turning into one hell of a lot bigger thing than I had come looking for. My job was to put a stop to the office machine rip-off in Beverly Hills, but that was only the tip of an iceberg. The Red Velvet Gang was operating in Hawaii, in the Far East, in Mexico, in Boston; name some other place, and you might be right. They were into narcotics and I didn't know what else. It was an international conspiracy, with its headquarters in the Red Velvet Snare in Hollywood.

And I was the only cop in the world who knew anything about it.

6

The Inside Caper

HARRY ANDREWS disappeared about six weeks after he got me into the Red Velvet Gang. He never said so long or anything; one day he just stopped showing up at headquarters.

"Goddammit, Franklin," he said to me about a week before he disappeared, "I got to get out of here. If at any time, now or later, they find out who you are and that I got you in, they'll kill me."

"Well," I said, "you probably won't be alone."

He said, "Yeah. Thanks a lot."

And one day Harry picked up his girlfriend and went somewhere and never came back. A couple of years later I picked up a teletype where he had been busted for residential burglary in San Diego, and with his rap sheet they probably put him away for a little while. But I never saw him again.

With Harry gone, I was the only one likely to get killed. I worried about that a little, wondering whether the whole caper was foolish on my part, but I couldn't let it bother me too much or I wouldn't be able to do my job. A scared cop is about as useful as boar tits.

My first plan was to get close to Ben Colt, and then I had
to find a way to work the snitch. If I got close to Ben, nobody was likely to make me for a cop because they all
figured that Ben couldn't be conned. Here he was, the leader
of one of the biggest, most successful criminal operations in
history, and he had never been arrested! Everybody else in
that gang had a rap sheet as long as a whore's dream, but the
only way I could come up with a picture of Ben was out of
San Francisco, where he had applied for some kind of business permit several years back and they had photographed
him.

Ben was one of the most likable guys I ever knew, and
that made my job both easier and harder. I really didn't
want to bust him. I admired the way he ran his business,
and I liked his style. It's funny, considering the advice that
Harry Andrews gave me, but Ben looked more like a construction worker than anybody I ever met. It wasn't the
way he dressed, which was casual but kind of classy. It was
the way he was. Ben was about five ten, 200 pounds, big-
boned frame with solid muscle on him, and a ruddy com-
plexion like an outdoor man. If you ran into him on the
street, you'd guess he tore tigers apart with his bare hands
for a living.

The first thing I impressed Ben with was my knowledge
of what was going on. One night we were sitting talking
with Joe Emmitson, one of the guys who were planning a
burglary up in Nichols Canyon, and he was worried about
the police patrol up that way.

"Okay," I said, "unless they have a special reason they
usually go up there once a day, in the daytime. Maybe twice
a week they'll roll through the canyon at night. Park someplace and watch for them, and if they come by at night,
you're probably safe the next night. But anytime you get
caught, it's tough titty because you got only two ways out
of that canyon on wheels."

Some of what I told them was true, and some I made up. I

didn't want them to know too much. But Ben Colt looked at me like I had the combination to the vault at the Bank of America. "Now how the hell would you know that?" he said.

"Ben," I said, "I worked those hills for years. I made it my business to find out things like that. I like to know the jurisdictions, the patrol routines, who works what, all that stuff. It's just business."

That kind of thing impressed Ben because he was all business himself. Take the car that Harry Andrews got busted in. It was Ben's car, which he had bought legally, but there was no way to trace it to him.

"For your personal use, go buy a nice car," Ben said. "But don't use it for work. For your jobs, buy a cheap car. What I do, I go to a car lot, or some guy who's selling it, and I pay maybe three hundred cash. Let them sign the pink slip over, but I never reregister it. Then if I'm on a job and the police crowd me, I can dump it, and there's no record that the car belongs to me."

"Damn!" I said. "I never thought of that. It could have saved me a lot of trouble." I figured it wouldn't make Ben mad if I flattered him a little; besides, it really was a pretty good trick.

Another time Black Rob and Vance Menard were sitting with us, drinking, and Ben said, "One night I'm with these two guys here and we stop off at some place down near Brawley, in the Imperial Valley. I checked into a motel and went to bed. I'm a businessman. But what do these clowns do? They go out on the town. They go out spending money and drinking and trying to carouse around with some of the girls, and the local police pull them over, and Black Rob has got some stolen stuff in the trunk of his car. They shake the car down, and both of them get busted. It shows how stupid they are."

He said this to me right in front of Black Rob and Menard, and they didn't do anything. Colt was the leader.

"Next morning," Colt said, "I go across into Mexico and pick up the load of narcotics I came for, and I come back and go on about my business. And these guys are in jail because they are not businessmen."

Colt was a careful drinker, too, a social drinker. He would sit there all night long in the Red Velvet Snare and drink just three beers, no more. Always Budweiser. He kept things under control, and he boasted to me that that was why he never got arrested.

After I had been in the gang a couple of months, I took to wearing a miniature sheriff's badge, a little star, on my belt. The guys at West Hollywood LASO, the sheriff's office for that area, seemed to think it was sacrilegious, but it didn't mean a thing. Old Gene Biscailuz and later Pete Pitchess used to hand those things out like Chinese fortune cookies until somebody raised a holler and stopped it. The guys in the gang just took it as a joke, and Colt kidded me about it; but all the same he was impressed.

It made an even bigger impression when I showed him my real badge. That was toward the end of that undercover job, which lasted for a whole year, a lot longer than anybody figured when it began. After about eight months Colt moved the gang's headquarters from the Red Velvet Snare to the Camelback Inn, down on Western Avenue. So many guys had been busted that he thought maybe the location had something to do with it. I had taken my picture out of the badge, so there was no ID that Colt could make, and I said, "Hey, Ben," and I pulled out the badge. "Look what I got."

"Where in the hell did you get that?" he wanted to know.

I said, "Never mind about where I got it. I got it."

Real fast he said, "I'll buy it from you!"

I wouldn't sell, but that son of a gun kept trying. He went all the way to $500.

"Jesus!" he said. "You must have a way of getting them. You can get another one." He figured that I had picked some detective's pocket or broke into his house because there are only two ways to get one of those badges: You can earn it, or you can steal it.

The way Ben ran that gang, he wanted action every night. There were about forty guys in it, all white except one, Glen Little. They didn't want anything to do with blacks, but they let this one guy in because he could peddle their narcotics in Watts and Compton. He was their Compton Connection.

Half a dozen of the guys were receivers. There was a phone on the wall at the rear end of the bar, and it was strictly a receiver's phone. The receivers would sit down at that end of the bar, and when that phone rang, one of them or maybe the owner, Curt, who also fenced, would answer it. Nobody else ever touched it. And the talk on that phone was always about jewelry or office machines or furs or narcotics.

They all were night people, and especially if they were out on a job, they wouldn't get to sleep until daybreak, so they drifted into the Red Velvet Snare one by one in late afternoon. About dark Ben Colt would meet with several of us at one of the tables, and he would ask Black Rob, "Well, what have we got going tonight?"

Black Rob was Colt's lieutenant, the number two guy. He might say, "Menard has a score to make."

"Who's he going to take with him?" Colt would say. He wanted to know all the details, and he'd tell them things to do or not to do. But he had somebody out on a job every damned night.

Colt got a cut off everything that came through the gang, in return for which he furnished leadership, bailout and legal protection. Colt was at the Red Velvet Snare, or later at the Camelback, almost all the time. When a guy got busted, as soon as he got his phone call, he'd call Colt, and Colt would have an attorney spring him.

"You got to have the right attorney," Ben told me. "No

good defense attorney will work without having some judge on his payroll.''

A guy would get busted at two o'clock in the morning, by three thirty he'd get a call in to Colt, by five o'clock the attorney would get a judge out of bed to sign a writ, and by six o'clock the guy would be out of jail.

It was also understood that you didn't have to worry much about a felony conviction. ''Your attorney gets you before the right judge, and you're home free,'' Colt said. ''You can always get a felony burglary reduced to misdemeanor, so instead of five to life you're looking at no worse than a hundred and eighty days in jail.'' And that was the way it worked out most of the time.

Manny Graber nearly laughed himself to death over a judge he went up before for arraignment after he got busted for burglary.

''Can you imagine that stupid son of a bitch?'' he said. ''He sets the date for the preliminary, and then he says to me, 'Mr. Graber, sir, would that be convenient for you? If it isn't, sir, just let the court know and we'll change it, sir. Hell, I never got 'sirred' so much in my life.''

Of course, the court has to accommodate the defendant to a reasonable degree, but there is never any worry whether it's convenient for the victim. The victim has no standing in court, and that's what Graber thinks is so goddamned funny.

While I was in the gang, the Supreme Court kicked out the death penalty, and those guys really tied on a celebration.

''Hey, man,'' Ben said, ''we don't have to worry about the cyanide pill anymore!''

They kept up on all the court rulings and the laws being made in Washington and Sacramento, and they were always worrying about going into a house or a building and having somebody come at them with a gun or a knife, and they'd have to kill the guy. It's not easy to get murder reduced to a misdemeanor.

Thcy all thought the courts were a joke, but in the whole year I lived with that gang I never heard one single word against the police. Anytime they called a cop a son of a bitch it was the same way cops use that term for each other. Said in a certain way, it doesn't mean anything. The thinking of a professional criminal when he gets busted is not to blame the police but to blame himself; he figures he made a mistake, and he plans not to do that again.

One word nobody in the Red Velvet Gang *ever* used for police is "pigs." That's a term used by left-wing radicals, but those professional criminals would never stoop so low.

They all liked the same music, mostly just two numbers. It seemed the jukebox was always playing either "Knock Three Times" or Johnny Cash's "Folsom Prison Blues." That first is a catchy semicountry tune about a guy and a gal, but the one they really liked was "Folsom Prison Blues." Except for Ben, they had every one been to prison, and the average guy who has done time associates himself with Johnny Cash because he sings about the plight of a poor downtrodden who goes to prison and then gets out and he's trying to make it. They never got tired of hearing that.

Another curious thing: They were a flag-waving bunch of good patriots, if you could overlook their occupation. We were deep in Vietnam them, and those guys were all for bombing Hanoi and killing the Vietcong and getting the war over by winning it. Every one of them was somewhere right of Barry Goldwater.

Once I got in with the bunch, I knew most of what was going on because I got close with Colt and I sat in on a lot of the meetings. Black Rob didn't like that much, but there wasn't anything he could do about it. And I learned things just by sitting around and listening to the guys talk. It was mostly shoptalk because thieves can't keep their mouths shut about their work. They can't go home and brag to their wives, they can't tell the minister, they can't talk about themselves on TV, so they tell each other what they did or what they're going to do. Every night the Red Velvet Snare was like a great big gaudy confessional.

When I knew about a job somebody was planning, I'd notify the jurisdiction where they were going, and if they could find him, they'd bust him. In addition to Beverly Hills, I worked mostly with LAPD's Wilshire and West LA divisions and with West Hollywood LASO, which has jurisdiction over the Sunset Strip and that county territory that runs right up against Beverly Hills. I'd phone them and give them a license number or a description, whatever information I had.

After the guys would leave the Red Velvet Snare to pull the job, I'd wait maybe half an hour, then stroll back to the pay phone in the rear hall next to the men's room. When you're drinking all evening, nobody thinks a thing of it if you go to the john now and then, and of course, nobody worried about me anyway because Colt trusted me. They never caught on because the phone call was the only thing that connected me with any of the busts; somebody else always made the arrest.

LAPD helped us get photos of the whole gang for ID purposes, and they did a fantastic job. We got the cooperation of a Von's supermarket across the street from the Red Velvet Snare, and the SIS unit—that's LAPD's Special Investigative Services—fixed some kind of long-lens camera setup on the roof. How they did it I don't know, but there was absolutely nothing showing.

They staked up there for a couple of weeks. Afternoons we'd go outside to get some fresh air, and I'd stand with my back to the street, so the guys talking to me would be facing the hidden camera, and those LAPD guys got mug shots as good as studio photographs. I'd look at them later and say,

"That's Colt, that's Black Rob, that's Menard," or whoever it was.

Sometimes I had to encourage things a little, which is what I did with Jake Farnum, a big fatso of about 300 pounds who was always moaning about having to pay some judge $3,000 a month to stay on the street. He had been busted five times in a row on five different break-ins, one of them at UCLA, where he got shot off a roof, and he was out on bail on all five jobs at the same time. He was paying through his attorney.

"Jake," I said one night, "how do you know the attorney isn't getting it all?"

And Jake said, "I don't. I'm afraid to try to find out."

I never did learn who the judge was or whether he was really on the take. But Jake's attitude was typical in that bunch. They figured that all judges are either crooked or stupid because that's the only way you can explain why they go so easy on professional criminals.

My thinking was that most likely it was Jake's attorney on the take, waiting to get all his money up front before going to trial. To get the money, he had to keep Jake on the street. The way it's done is with a code word all the judges know about, the name of a nonexistent witness. The code changes every month or so; when I first heard of it, the name was "Mrs. Green."

How it works is the lawyer asks for a postponement, telling the judge, "Your Honor, I have been unable to locate an important witness for the defense, Mrs. Green." He wants time to find her.

Now the judge, who usually has been a defense lawyer himself, knows the code, and he knows that there is no Mrs. Green in this case. What the lawyer is really telling him is: "I haven't got my money from the defendant up front yet, so I want him to remain on bail another couple of weeks so he can rip off some more people until he gets enough to pay me. *Then* I'll be ready to go to trial."

The judge says okay, and it isn't a payoff. It's worse. It's the court turning itself into a collection agency for the defense lawyer and conspiring with him to promote the commission of more crimes. The legal profession knows about this, but the legal profession practically never does anything about cleaning up its own house, no matter what they say; the way the bar looks at it, almost the only crime a lawyer can commit is stealing a client's money.

So with Jake having to come up with $3,000 a month on top of living expenses, he was always looking for something to do. I found him something. I was talking with another guy in the group, Bus Markham, and he was bragging to me because he thought I was a hijacker, which is pretty high society in the criminal blue book.

"Man," Bus said, "we're loaded! We got a whole truckload of stuff, and we got to find a sucker."

In that group a sucker was a buyer, a receiver. Bus and a buddy, Streeter Long, had ripped off a leather and suede shop on Hollywood Boulevard.

I said, "Well, I know somebody that might be interested. I'll fill him in."

Later I was having a drink with Jake Farnum, and I mentioned these two guys who had a lot of leather and suede.

"I got to talk to them," Jake said.

The next night Bus came over to me and bought me a drink. "Thanks a lot," he said. "I made the deal, I got the sucker to set up for me, he's going to meet us tonight, and we'll deliver the stuff for cash."

Bus hung around for a while, and pretty soon Jake Farnum came in. I knew they couldn't make the switch until they both left the place. Finally, they went out, a couple of minutes apart, and I made my phone call. I gave them the number of Jake's station wagon, and I said, "Wherever he goes, just stay with him. He's going to make this buy."

Jake picked up a partner, a guy named Kirk Russell who

had an address in Canoga Park but really lived in Hollywood, and they went out the Hollywood Freeway to Barham Boulevard and down Barham into Burbank, and they
met Bus and Streeter on a little side street where they had
parked their truck with the stuff in it.

LAPD Criminal Conspiracy picked them up and followed
them all the way. They moved in just as Jake was paying
out $5,000 for the load, and they grabbed the guys and they
took the money as evidence.

That ended Jake staying on the streets. Whoever was
helping him figured that Jake's business was small time,
but this looked like maybe even hijacking was involved,
and a lot of money, and that put Jake in the big time. His
friend backed off, and Jake got five to life. If what he told me
about the judge was true, I saved him $3,000 a month. But I
doubt that he would be grateful.

The only Red Velvet Gang bust that I actually went along
on was one that West Hollywood LASO wanted. They had
the teeth grinds because of too many rip-offs, and Cork let
them use me because there was no other way they could
work it.

They handled it like the Normandy invasion. They put in
seven ground units, which is fourteen men, plus two choppers on standby at Parker Center, and they set up a command post in a room in the crummy little hotel across the
street from the Camelback. They had all that, and me.

After a couple of hours Herb Jameson decided to go out
and pull a job. Herb was the biggest pusher of narcotics in
the San Fernando Valley. He was taking a couple of people
along on the job, Miki Tikori, who was one of the regular
girls in the gang, and Rudy Acosta, not the actor, but a Mexican wetback.

They went out to their car, and I came out and crossed
the street, ducked down an alley to the back of the hotel
and into the command post. Two deputies who worked as a

team were in there; one was a foxy little redheaded chick, and the other was a horny guy who was always trying to get his partner into bed.

"Okay," I said, "two guys and a gal just came out. They're getting in that red car on the side street."

They radioed a chopper to get airborne, and the guy said, "We'll shut down here and help tail them. Why don't you come along?"

I figured I could be useful, especially if we lost them and had to pick them up again, so I got in the backseat. They were both up front. We followed Herb's car up Western to the Hollywood Freeway and out to the Valley. We were in Cahuenga Pass when the chopper got over us, and he said, "Okay, spot the car for me."

The way you do that, you get directly behind the car and turn on your turn indicator, but you don't change lanes.

"I got him," the chopper said.

And we dropped off. From the radio we knew they kept on the Hollywood Freeway to the Ventura Freeway, west to the San Diego Freeway, then north to the Burbank Boulevard off ramp.

"Hell," I said, "they're headed for Herb's apartment. He lives at Sepulveda and Magnolia." Sure enough, they went into the garage there, and we staked out the place with several units.

The two deputies and I got by a parkway at the end of the alley. We sat there for about half an hour, and a guy came walking out of the alley.

"It's Jameson!" I whispered to the two in front. I ducked down, because I shouldn't be seen, and it was a bright moonlight night.

Jameson looked across the street at our car, and he acted like he thought maybe it was a detective car. He started to walk our way.

The male deputy, who was always looking for an excuse,

grabbed the female deputy and began kissing her and pulling her blouse open, and she was fighting him. She said, "Come on, now, you son of a bitch!"

"Duty," he said, "is duty." And he got his hand in there on her tit.

"Get your goddamned hand out of my brassiere!" she said. "You're going beyond the call of duty!"

All this was in whispers, and I was in the back trying not to break up, but Jameson saw the girl being half undressed and that looked all right, so he walked away. It worked.

Jameson went to an old white car at the curb, leaned into it, then backed out and went to his pad. Pretty soon the red car came back out. The chopper, which can only stay up about two hours, had refueled at Van Nuys, and we got him on the car again. We had a ground unit investigate the old white car.

In about ten minutes the ground unit came back on the air and said, "Anybody need a fix?" They had found a complete hype kit taped under the dash. That old white car was one of Jameson's stash cars, and somebody was supposed to drop by and pick up the kit, probably before going to pull a job.

We followed Herb back into Hollywood, to an apartment complex on Franklin Avenue. They parked in front, and the two guys went in, leaving the girl in the car. In a few minutes Herb and the wetback came out, carrying a beautiful big color television set, a console. They put it in the trunk, had to leave the trunk lid up, and pulled out into traffic. We radioed for a beat unit to pull them over.

Seven units, two choppers, a command post setup, and the only thing they were stealing this night was a television set! That's like sending the First Armored Division to get rid of some gophers. But that wasn't as bothersome as what happened after the arrest, which was par for the pros: Jameson and his friends got out of jail within twenty-four hours.

Worst of all, I guess, is the uneasy feeling you get about a case with loose ends that you can't tie up. That happened to me with Angelita Garcia.

Angelita was a good-looking, dark-eyed little chick I got friendly with in the Camelback Inn. She was about half Spanish or Mexican, maybe twenty-three to twenty-five years old, and she interested me because I could tell that she hated the ground all those guys walked on, but I couldn't figure why. Her boyfriend was Vance Menard, who was a big narcotics middleman who bought in Mexico and delivered to pushers in LA, and she acted like she hated Vance more than anybody else.

"Go to hell, Vance!" she told him one night when he was trying to get her to stop drinking. She was sitting and talking with me, and she had had a couple of tequilas with strawberry pop, which would make anybody throw up, but she was also a hype, which makes it dangerous.

"Look, Angie," he said, grabbing her by the arm, "you got to get something to eat. Come on." He was trying to get her over to the food bar.

She jerked her arm away. "*You* eat," she said. "I don't feel like it."

"Dammit!" he said. "With the stuff you're on you can't drink like that!"

She said, "That's very funny, coming from you, shithead."

"You'll kill yourself," Vance said, which was true.

And she said, "Yeah, and I can just see this whole bunch of dirty bastards laughing themselves silly. Go bother somebody else."

Everything she said to those guys or about them came out like a snarl, especially when she talked to Vance, the guy she was sleeping with. It didn't make sense.

Vance was always making trips to Mexico to pick up stuff, and Angelita usually went along. I suggested to Vance that I'd like to go with them sometime and make a good connection down there myself. He didn't fall all over himself with enthusiasm, but Angelita liked the idea of having company, so he said okay. I didn't really give a damn about his Mexican Connection; what I wanted to know was who up here bought the stuff from Vance.

We met in the dirt parking lot of a little beer joint on Sunset at closing time, two o'clock in the morning. It was a crummy little place that would look run-down in East LA, where everything looks run-down. We took off from there, and we stopped only to eat or get gas or water the personnel. We drove down through Nogales into Mexico, to a ranch outside San Luis which is owned by Jesus Arboles. Arboles is a Mexican federal agent, a narcotics dealer, and one of the dirtiest double-cross artists on either side of the border. The Mexican government should make a monument to him as an example of their corruption.

Arboles grew his own marijuana on that ranch; he harvested it, baled it, and sold it to dealers like Vance. We pulled into his barn and loaded the trunk up with 200 kilos. He must have had 5,000 kilos stacked in that barn.

We had a beer and tacos served up by a quiet, scared-looking woman in a big dirty kitchen, and there was a lot of palaver in Spanish, the general drift of which sounded like directions for getting back into the States without getting caught. Arboles kept repeating, *"El camino con roca al derecha,"* the road with the rocks or cliff on the right.

And we took off again. We had now been on the road for about twenty-four hours, and we had started after a full day. Angelita curled up in the backseat and went to sleep.

I said, "I thought maybe we'd spend the night."

"No," Vance said. "Not there. We stop when we get back to the States."

The road was dirt, and pretty soon we came to a fork, and Vance went to the right. In a little while I could see the land to the left of us start rising. It was a tilted mesa, and it got higher and higher until it was a big cliff.

"Hey, Vance," I said, "I thought Arboles said to go on the other side of that thing."

Vance pulled out a gun and laid it handy on the seat between us. "I know all the ways around here," he said. "I never go where Jesus says. It's probably a trap. Half his customers get waylaid between the ranch and the border." He didn't say anything for a while, and then he added, "But maybe he learned his lesson. Last month his nephew Luis got killed trying to rip off a customer. Luis was only seventeen. They shot him. But you can't trust Jesus; the son of a bitch is a goddamned crook!"

If Arboles had anybody waiting to ambush us, they waited in the wrong place. We had no trouble at all. Finally, Vance turned off the road, and we bounced across open desert for a while until we came to a barbed-wire fence. Vance got a pair of wire cutters out of the trunk, clipped the wire and pulled it back, and we drove through the fence.

"Welcome to the United States," he said. And he put his gun away.

"That was the border?"

"That's all it is for several hundred miles along here, a barbed-wire fence. This is where Jesus said to cross."

I said, "I thought you didn't take his advice."

"Oh, this is different," Vance said. "He'll have his own customers ripped off, but he doesn't want to get a bad reputation letting them get caught by the border patrol. He gets his information straight from the Mexican police, and when he says it's safe here tonight, that means there isn't a helicopter or muleback patrol or anything within about fifty miles."

I kept looking for landmarks. We got onto a road, and after a while we passed a sign: DANGER. U.S. MILITARY FIRING RANGE. DO NOT ENTER. FIRING AT ALL HOURS.

Vance didn't even slow down. "Hey," I said, "what about that warning?"

"It's all bluff," Vance said. "No firing tonight. But maybe by morning."

We drove on across the firing range, and then we hit a main highway and turned south again, back into Nogales, and we got rooms in a motel. Vance and Angelita had one room; I had another.

There was a little coffee shop next to the motel. I walked in there about eleven o'clock in the morning, and there was Angelita having breakfast, but no Vance. "Still sleeping," she told me.

"I thought he'd want to get going," I said.

She shook her head. "We can't. It's not time yet."

"What do you mean, 'not time'?"

"There's an agricultural inspection station up by the Salton Sea," she said. "We can't hit that until two o'clock this afternoon."

Those stations are run by the California Department of Agriculture on all the main roads into the state, to keep out fruits and vegetables that might be diseased or carrying insect pests. They shake down most of the cars, and they confiscate anything that's on a prohibited list, like Florida oranges. I hadn't thought about the problem of getting 200 kilos of grass past that inspection.

I said, "Isn't there a better way?"

And she said, "Oh, it's safe enough. But it's safer by air. Bill Carpenter brings it in that way, but only after he takes a load of office machines to Mexico City. He didn't have a trip right now. Anyway, Vance always likes to drive. I don't think he wants to give anyone else a chance to get his hands on the stuff. He doesn't trust anybody."

I had to be careful about pressing, but she felt like talking, and I got some details out of her. Coming back north, they'd land at the Mexican airport near Nogales and load up with narcotics. They'd file a flight plan, say, to Phoenix. They'd fly across the border as low as possible, to stay un-

der the border patrol radar, and when they were well inside
the United States, they'd radio that they were having engine trouble and they'd land at some little desert airstrip
where there was no customs agent and nobody was expecting them.

Nobody, that is, except a guy with a car who would pick
up the narcotics and head for LA. Then Carpenter would
take off again and fly to Phoenix and get a clean bill of inspection. That's how most of those illegal narcotics flights
operate; all it takes is a good pilot to fly under the radar,
which is where the crashes happen.

I kept hoping Vance would stay in bed, because this was
the first chance I'd had to talk to Angelita without some of
the guys around.

"What do you get out of all this, anyway?" I said.

She shrugged. "It's something to do."

I said, "Well, it's none of my business, but you sure don't
seem to like Vance very well for a guy you're shacking
with."

She looked out the window for a minute and took a long
drag on her cigarette. Finally, she said, "Vance is a bastard!
That whole bunch are bastards! I hate them all!" Her voice
was so low I could hardly hear her, but it had an edge like a
hacksaw.

I said, "Most of them seem like pretty good guys. They
treat you girls okay, don't they?"

The look she gave me could torch a hole through a vault
door. "What's that got to do with anything?" she wanted to
know. "Do you know what they did to my husband?"

I said, "I didn't even know you were married."

And she said, "I'm not. Not anymore. Those bastards
killed him!" Her color was hot, there was sweat on her upper lip, and she looked like she wanted to blow up the
world. Then all of a sudden her shoulders sagged, and the
fire went out. She went on talking, very quietly now. "Tom
was a beautiful man. One of those clean-cut guys, an Anglo.

He was going to be an electrical engineer. We had only been married about a year. Then we got in with that dirty bunch, and they got us on dope."

She didn't say anything more, and finally, I said, "What happened?"

"He OD'd."

So that was it. I waited a minute, and then I said, "If you hate those guys, why do you hang around?"

And she said, "I don't know anything else to do. If I wasn't with them, I'd be with another bunch just like them."

At least, I had my answers.

About an eighth of a mile short of the agricultural inspection station Vance pulled over to the side of the road, got out a pair of binoculars and studied the setup. Finally he said, "It's okay. He's in the right lane."

We drove on up, into the right lane, and the uniformed agent leaned in the car and said, "Are you carrying any fruits, vegetables, cotton, agricultural products of any kind?"

"I'm coming from Mike's place," Vance said.

The guy looked at Vance, and he looked at me and Angelita, and he looked back at Vance, and he said, "Okay, you can go on."

We were home free. Just come from Mike's place, and there is no inspection. Back in LA I notified the agriculture people, and later they told me they had taken care of the guy; I don't know what they did with him, but there was no way it could be connected to me.

Late that night we got back to the crummy little beer joint where we had started the trip, and Vance said to me, "Okay, get out."

I said, "What do you mean, get out?"

"I'm making a delivery," he said. "I can't take you with me."

Angelita was right; Vance didn't trust anybody. He drove

off with the girl, and it all happened too fast for me to get a
tail on him.

For maybe a month I debated about Angelita, and I decided to take a chance on her. I took her to lunch at Paul's
Steak House on Burton Way, and we had a couple of drinks,
and finally, I laid my badge on her.

"I'm a cop," I said. "I'm after those guys."

She didn't seem surprised. It was like okay, this happens
three times a day, so what? Sometimes hypes get like that.

"The guy I want," I said, "is not Vance. It's the guy he de-
livers to. Where did you go that night?"

She didn't know exactly, but she told me what she could
remember. "We went straight out Sunset," she said, "past
the Beverly Hills Hotel, and we made a right turn through
an archway." That would be the main gate into Bel Air.
"We went straight up a winding road for a mile or two."
How you do that I don't know, but it was a woman talking.

"We turned off to the right," she said, "and we came to an
iron gate that was locked. Vance knew how to signal the
people, and the gate opened, and we went up a long driveway, and he parked the car in a big garage that had space for
five or six cars. We went inside, and it was the most beautiful home I ever saw. And we had coffee with the man."

"Did you get his name?" I said.

"Oh, yes," she said. "Vance introduced me. He was Joe
Ricco. He was very nice. And then another man came in, a
Mr. Carlino, and he told Vance that he wanted to have the
next shipment."

"Ricco," I said. "What did he look like?"

"Well, he was, I guess, maybe sixty years old. White-
haired."

Joe Ricco was the big narcotics dealer for West LA and
that area. He was about sixty and white-haired.

"Okay, fine," I said. "Will you do something for me? Will
you show me where Vance drove you that night? Do you
think you can remember that well?"

"I'll try," she said.

We drove into Bel Air, and we wound around on those streets that curl like a nest of snakes, and suddenly Angelita said, "God! That looks just like the place!"

It was Lou Farnsworth's old place, a fifteen-acre estate behind an electrified fence. I had been there many times. Lou was a friend of mine, although he didn't know that I was a cop. A call girl of our mutual acquaintance once told me, "Lynn, don't let on that you're a cop. Lou is straight, but it would just kind of dampen things." So Lou thought that I worked as a public relations man for the Beverly Hills Hotel. Lou has nothing to do with crime; he is a Texan who made it big in farm implements, and he owns several factories in Texas. One of his good friends was President Lyndon Johnson.

By the time this caper was pulled Lou had sold the place to a publisher whose name is a household word. Maybe it's a bedroom word. But I wasn't interested in busting Bedroom Word; he is a dingaling, but that is not a crime, and there was always a chance that he didn't know what was going on in his own house. The guy I wanted was Ricco.

Besides, Angelita wasn't sure she had fingered the right place. "I'd rather do it at night," she said, "like it was with Vance. Then I think I could be sure."

I took her into the station and introduced her to Wayne Rutherford, and we set up a date for the three of us to meet that night and go over the whole route again, beginning at the beer joint on Sunset. We parted friends.

Angelita didn't keep the appointment. She never came back to the Camelback; I never saw her again; I never found a trace of her. I think she got scared and skipped.

I hope that's all that happened.

7

Suspicion

AFTER ANGELITA disappeared, I had to wonder if I had been burned. If she had told Vance or anybody else in the gang that I was a cop, Ben Colt would collect my ticket. I got a little nervous, and I began to be very careful around those guys. I stayed out of the alleys around the Camelback, and in the place I always sat with my back to a wall.

Of course, getting burned had been something to worry about that whole year undercover, but at first I didn't exactly realize the chance I was taking. One thing I did was a little risky: As soon as I got photos, I posted Ben's and Black Rob's on the station bulletin board, and the license numbers of their cars, with the understanding that any unit that rousted those guys was never to mention me. What didn't occur to me was that Ben was the kind of guy who might come into the Beverly Hills station just to look around and chat with people and check whether we knew anything about him. Later, when I was working the ski-mask bandit case, that's exactly what happened, but in that case I wasn't working undercover.

When I posted those photos, Bill Steen and Larry Leffler were working my old Beat 9, and they drove Ben Colt and

Black Rob crazy. Every time those two would come down
Wilshire or Robertson looking for a place to hit Steen and
Leffler would pull them over, search their car, FI them and
just generally hassle them.

"Jesus Christ!" Ben said. "Goddammit! Shit! Those Beverly Hills policemen, they won't let you turn around. They
won't let you drive down their goddamned streets. Any
time you try it, the sons of bitches roust you."

Many a day I walked into the station in the morning, and
I'd run into Steen and Leffler, and they'd laugh and say,
"Hey, we shook your friends last night."

And I'd say, "Yeah, I already heard all about it."

After a while the guys stayed out of Beverly Hills. Colt
was no fool. He knew something was going, and when he
saw anything like that, he'd tell the guys, "Lay off it." Pretty soon they stayed out of Beverly Hills most of the time,
which was what I wanted. First, I wanted to get them out of
my town, which was what I was paid for, and next, I wanted
to bust the whole gang.

To arrest somebody and make it stick, you've got to catch
them on the job. Wayne Rutherford's idea was for me to go
in with them, like I did that one time, and to get caught
with them. Wayne is a good cop, but he doesn't have a lot of
street experience.

"I'll walk you off to the side to quiz you," Wayne said,
"and you slug me—slug me good—and you get away on
foot."

"Wayne," I said, "no way. They'll smell it, and they'll
kill me."

Wayne made the mistake of running it by the DA, and
the DA said the same thing for another reason. "Entrapment," he said. "No way."

The first time I almost got burned it was one of those
things you figure can't happen. I was going out to case a job
in downtown LA, and Ben Colt and Black Rob were riding
with me. So I went to Tom Edmonds, a sergeant who works

auto theft and who always keeps two or three license plates around in case of need.

"Tom," I said, "I need a cold plate."

He gave me a Nevada plate, which I put on my car. Now I was driving down the Hollywood Freeway with Ben and Black Rob, it was nighttime, and maybe I got careless; but suddenly the Chippies—the California Highway Patrol—pulled me over, lights flashing.

"Just sit tight," I told the guys. "I'll take care of this."

I went back to talk to the cop. It was a little touchy, with the phony plate and two worried guys in the car, one with a gun and the other with Mace, and I had to deal with this Chippie. Nobody knows what a Chippie is going to do, and they get killed a lot because they don't follow normal procedures. I've seen a Chippie walk up to a car he has stopped with a pencil in one hand and his ticket book in the other; he could write a ticket faster than he could draw his gun. I've seen two of them walk up together, instead of one hanging back right rear where he can watch everything. The guy is a traffic violator, but you never know whether the reason he did something wrong was that he just robbed a bank. If you have your holster unsnapped and your hand on your gun and he turns out to be a minister, you can always apologize and let him know you pray a lot.

The guy met me halfway between the cars and said, "Let's see your driver's license."

I showed him my driver's license, and he said, "Let's see the registration on the car."

I got it out of the glove box and came back and showed it to him. And he said, "You have a California registration, and you have a Nevada plate on there."

"Oh," I said, "I'm sorry, my real plate's in the trunk of the car." I started to pop the trunk lid.

He said, "What do you mean, your real plate's in the trunk?" And he grabbed me and put me over the trunk and threw the cuffs on me.

"Listen!" I said in a loud whisper. "Don't burn this! I'm working on an undercover job, and I'm sorry, but my real plate *is* in the trunk of the car, and these plates I'm using are cold. Call my station; you'll find out."

He said, "You just sit tight." He had his gun out now, and he backed up to his car, and he pulled out the radio mike and asked for a make on the Nevada plate.

The goddamned plate was stolen! And I am hip deep in shit. He called for a backup unit because he was going to take all three of us in.

"Hey, call Lieutenant Princeton in Beverly Hills," I said. "He's on the desk. Tell him you have Lynn Franklin, and he'll tell you I'm working an undercover deal. But, dammit, don't burn me with these two guys!"

The Chippie was reasonable. He said, "Okay, I'll try it." He radioed his desk to check with Lieutenant Princeton, and pretty soon the word came back.

"Never heard of him," was what Princeton said! That son of a bitch and I had been having problems because he was strictly an eight-to-four cop, which in my book is no cop at all, but he had no cause to try to burn me, and he was in violation of his oath. I knew that Colt had a gun, and Black Rob his can of Mace, and this Chippie didn't know what was going on. Princeton could have got us both killed.

It took awhile, but I got the Chippie to make one more call. I said, "Look, I'm sure you've run into this kind of stuff. Lieutenant Princeton hates my guts, which is mutual. Talk to somebody else. Call Chief Cork, get the dispatcher, talk to anybody, but don't burn me! These guys are dangerous!"

Finally, he got Captain Rutherford, and Wayne said, "Hell, yes, he's working undercover! Don't burn him!"

So the Chippie took the cuffs off me, and he chewed me out beside the car, where Colt and Black Rob got an earful, and he put me back in the car, and we drove away.

"What the hell was that all about?" Ben said.

"Ah, they got my license screwed up some way," I said. "He thought it was stolen, but they finally got it straightened out. But can you imagine that son of a bitch? He blames me when it's the goddamned DMV that fucked it up!"

That satisfied them. But we didn't case any jobs that night. The next day I had a little talk with Tom Edmonds about his goddamned cold plate. What had happened was that when he ran it, it came out cold because it wasn't reported stolen until later. They ought to run those things every time before they hand them out.

Another time I almost got burned involved a little French girl named Michele I busted for prostitution at the Beverly Wilshire Hotel. Later I developed Michele into a snitch. But sometimes a prostitute turned snitch can be a pain in the ass, especially if she gets the idea you like her. Michele came through for me many times, but she got possessive, just like I was a boyfriend. I couldn't shake her of the idea that something might be going with us, and she always wanted to know everyplace I went and everything I did.

One night I was sitting in the Red Velvet Snare with the guys, drinking and carrying on, and Michele just happened to walk in. She saw me and came over, and just to be funny she called me by my last name, which was lucky; Franklin sounds enough like Franko that nobody noticed.

"Oh, Franklin," she said, pouting, "so this is where you're hanging out now. I was wondering why I never see you around Beverly Hills anymore."

I grabbed her and took her over to a corner table by ourselves, and I bought her a drink. I shoveled some quarters into the jukebox to make noise, and I said, "Look, Michele, you got to keep your big mouth shut, and you got to stay out of here!"

"Why?" she said. "Just so you can make it with somebody? You're slipping around!"

"What's it to you if I was?" I said.

She stuck her lower lip out, and she said, "I thought it was me you liked."

"Sure I like you," I said. "But I'm not strung out over you or anybody else."

She wouldn't listen; she was stuck on that one note. "I know what you're doing," she said, "you're trying to pick that up." She pointed to some gal sitting at the bar who just happened to be looking over at us.

"Jesus Christ!" I said. "I'll pick up a fatal disease if you don't pay attention. If these people find out I'm a cop, they're going to kill me! Can't you get that through your goddamned head?"

I had one hell of a time convincing her, but finally I got her off that bandwagon. "Okay," I said. "Now get your ass out of here, and keep it out."

She did.

By the time that Ben Colt moved headquarters out of the Red Velvet Snare and down to the Camelback, he knew there was a snitch in the gang. Everybody did, and as one guy after another got busted, everybody got edgy. But nobody suspected me because I was so close to Colt.

"Okay, so who the hell is it?" Black Rob said one night. He was one of the guys I had to worry the most about, because he was one tough bastard, and he didn't like me for bull piss; he thought I was trying to edge him out of the number two spot in the group.

Vance Menard said, "Well, it wasn't Jake Farnum." Everybody laughed, but it wasn't funny laughter.

"Yeah," Colt said. "It wasn't Artie Bumpus. It wasn't Skow Pucinski. It wasn't Jim Leffingwell." He kept on naming guys who had been busted on the job since I went to work on that bunch, and finally, he said, "It's probably somebody sitting here in this bar right now."

For a minute or two things got very quiet and uncomfortable. The jukebox wasn't going, and nobody was talking, and everybody was looking at everybody else, and you could almost hear the suspicion growing, like corn in July.

Suddenly there was a commotion by the front entrance and a couple of guys in white outfits, ambulance attendants, came running in.

"Where's the guy?" one of them said.

"What guy?" said Les Waffel, the owner of the Camelback.

"The guy that's hurt. We got a call."

Manny Graber was just coming out from the men's room, and he said, "Back here." He took the ambulance people back into the hallway. In a minute one of them went outside and came back with a stretcher, and they carried out a guy by the street name of Matt. I never did learn his real name; in that group if you pressed for a real name, they started looking funny at you. Matt was bloody and unconscious, and it looked like he had been pistol whipped and stomped.

"What happened?" Colt asked Graber.

"I don't know," Graber said. "I guess somebody thought he was the snitch."

"Who the hell called the ambulance?" Les Waffel wanted to know.

Graber said he did. "I found him back there," he said. "I put in a call."

"Goddammit, Graber!" Les said. "You ought to have more fucking sense than that! You start calling an ambulance every time some bastard gets beat up, and the cops will get interested. I don't want those guys nosing around here. No more fucking ambulances, see?"

"Okay, okay," Graber said. He was a little teed off.

Ben Colt said, "Matt is just small time. I think they got the wrong guy."

I figured that it was Harvey Krawczyk who had beat up on Matt. Krawczyk was a part-time bartender just out of Folsom Prison, a hard-nosed bandit who always carried a .45 and wouldn't mind using it. The first time I tried to get him busted he and Joe Donoris went out on an early-evening job, and I phoned the tip to West Hollywood LASO.

When they didn't show up again by about one o'clock in the morning, I felt pretty sure LASO had grabbed them.

I was feeling good about that and having a little fun with Krawczyk's girlfriend, a cute little blonde named Alice who liked to tease the guys sexually. She was always making suggestive remarks, and she made sure that you got a good look at her tits and her thighs, which were worth looking at.

Alice and I were sitting up at the bar, having a drink together. She had kicked her shoes off, and she had laid both her legs across my lap, and her side-slit dress kept slipping open so that every now and then I got a glimpse of her pink lace bikini panties, and we were talking and laughing and having a big time.

All of a sudden Krawczyk was standing there between us, taking all this in. "What the hell is going on here?" he said.

I let her legs slip off my lap, and I moved over one stool, so he could move in and sit next to Alice. I knew better than to play around with somebody else's girl, but I thought he was in jail. LASO had goofed; they got Joe Donoris, but Krawczyk got away.

He got away like that more than once. Another time was when he went out on a job with Kent Blackman and Manny Graber and Miki Tikori. I phoned LASO, and they found the car parked alongside an office building off Beverly Boulevard. Miki was sitting in it, waiting, and they grabbed her. Just inside the door, which had a stripped lock, they found ten IBM machines stacked up ready to load into the car. They got Graber and Blackman, but Krawczyk crawled out a window or hid in the building or something, and he got away.

A couple of hours later I was sitting at the bar, and in walked Krawczyk, and I knew something had gone wrong. But this time I wasn't taking any more chances playing games with Alice. I was just sitting up there next to a quiet little guy known as Little John Markey, minding my own business.

Krawczyk came back and stopped just past me. He reached over between me and Little John, grabbed Little John's bottle of Coors and cracked it over the bar. I got ready to move fast. Krawczyk grabbed Little John by the hair, jerked his head back and said, "You snitching son of a bitch, you!"

And he took that broken bottle and ripped Little John's throat from ear to ear.

Little John never said a word. He fell off his stool, and he just lay there on the floor, pumping blood all over. Krawczyk threw the broken bottle down into the blood, stepped up to the bar again, and very calm, he said to Les Waffel, "Gimme a beer, I'm thirsty."

"Call an ambulance!" somebody yelled.

And Les Waffel said, "No goddamned ambulance! Just get him out of here!"

Ben Colt and Black Rob picked up Little John and carried him out to Black Rob's car. I followed them. They threw Little John into the trunk, and we got in and took off.

Black Rob drove down to Queen of Angels Hospital, and he and Ben lifted Little John out of the trunk and tossed him onto the lawn. We went to a filling station about three blocks away, and Black Rob gave the phone a dime and called the hospital.

"Hey," he said, "you got a patient out on the lawn. Take a look." And he hung up, and we went back to the Camelback.

About two months later Little John walked into the Camelback one afternoon and sat down at the bar and ordered a Coors, just like nothing had happened. His right arm is paralyzed; Krawczyk cut a nerve somewhere that left the arm dead. But Little John never said a word about that incident, and neither did Krawczyk or anybody else.

It was Manny Graber calling the ambulance for Matt that got some of the guys to wondering about Manny. He was the next guy to get it after Little John. He lived in an apartment on Sunset, and one night a couple of guys kicked the door in and stomped the living hell out of him. They put him in the hospital. He wouldn't say who they were, but I'm pretty sure one of them was Krawczyk, because Krawczyk liked to think of himself as the enforcer.

About a month later Graber was well again, and he went up to the rooftop restaurant at 9000 Sunset, on the Strip. Krawczyk followed him up there, walked in on him while he was eating his lunch, pulled out his .45 and blew Graber's guts out all over the table.

Graber lived, but he doesn't have the guts he used to have. Krawczyk got away clean. I finally got him busted for robbery, but I never did anything about the beatings or the beer bottle slashing or the shooting. I wasn't in the group to prevent them trying to kill each other.

But all this stuff bothered Chief Cork. I had been in the Red Velvet Gang for a year now, and my luck was running good; but luck doesn't last forever, and he knew it.

"I want you to get out of there," Cork said. "When you went in with that group, the loss was running around six million a year. Now it's down to almost zero. Get out of there!"

I said, "Cork, I can't just up and walk out. If one guy does not show up some night at the Camelback, the rumors start flying. They figure that guy must be the snitch. If I walk out, I'm the snitch."

"Now, look," Cork said, "I don't know how you do it, but you get the hell out of it! I wake up at night with a call, and before I can pick up the phone, I'm in a cold sweat. Some night they're going to tell me Franklin's got his ass blown off."

I started trying to figure a way, but getting out of undercover work is like jumping off a tall building: There isn't any good place to quit.

It was maybe a week later that Ben Colt laid something interesting on me. He was going back to Boston with a load of grass, and he was driving because he had people to see along the way. I thought I could make use of that.

"If you got a good connection," Ben told me, "I can come up with twenty-five thousand to buy grass, anytime. Just give me a couple of hours."

Suddenly Roger Bedford and Joe Langer walked in and sat down at the bar. I was surprised to see them because they weren't supposed to come around.

A couple more minutes, and Bruce Campbell, my old partner, and Ed Zenter came walking in. I thought, *What the fuck is this?* They walked down the bar and around between the tables and out of my view. I had my chair leaned back to a wall with an outside corner, but there was a blind spot on my left side.

All of a sudden somebody kicked my chair out from under me, and as I went down, he kicked me again in the face and knocked me back against the wall. I figured, *All hell's to pay now!* and I went for my gun. Now I could see it was Campbell on me. He kicked the gun out of my hand and stomped me a couple of times.

At the bar Bedford had yelled out, "Police officers! Everybody freeze!" He and Langer had their guns out, and everybody was frozen.

Campbell and Zenter jerked me up, and my nose was bleeding where Campbell had kicked me. There is a way to kick a guy, hit him with your instep exactly the way you kick a football, and it will slam him around, but it won't bruise him or cut the skin. Campbell hadn't done it right, and I was a little beat up. They called me a few names, put the cuffs on me and marched me outside. And all this happened a lot quicker than I can tell it.

They put me in a car, and we headed for Beverly Hills, and after we had gone a couple of blocks, Campbell took the cuffs off me and said, "Okay, now you're out of that bunch."

Cork was waiting at the station in his office, and he said, "It was the only safe way we could figure, so I put Campbell in charge of it. Now I got something else I want you to work on. But before you come in tomorrow, get a haircut."

My hair was growing a little long because most of the
guys in the gang let their hair grow a little. I said, "I like it
this way."

And Cork said, "Get a haircut!"

"Okay."

And Campbell and I walked out of the office. When we
got outside, I hauled off and slapped him in the face. I got
him good and knocked him down to the floor. And I said,
"If you were going to kick me so hard, you could have done
it right."

I got thirty-eight guys in that gang busted. I even got Colt
arrested for the first time in his life, after I was out of the
gang, because he had told me he was driving back to Boston.
I got him busted in Ohio, where they have the toughest narcotics laws in the country, and he's doing five to life.

But most of them went right back on the streets. You
could tell by their rap sheets that they didn't stay long in
jail. Most of them had been arrested eight or a dozen times,
Black Rob and several others as many as sixteen times, and
Vance Menard had been busted thirty-two times.

No honest citizen is ever going to get arrested ten or
twenty or thirty times, most of them on felony charges. It
can't happen if you're straight. And the only way it can happen to a professional criminal is if the courts keep turning
him loose to commit more crimes. Bill Carpenter, the guy
with the jet service, had a two-page rap sheet with eleven
entries for narcotics, hijacking and a fine assortment of
crimes. For all of which he once got eleven months in jail,
and another time he got six consecutive *weekends* in jail!
That was his total penalty for twenty-five years of crime.
Rap sheets like that are proof that the courts are not protecting society.

So I broke up the Red Velvet Gang, but with damned little help from the courts I couldn't expect to do it by getting
those guys put away.

Suspicion did it. All the busts got everybody so distrustful of everybody else that they quit doing business with each other. The gang just broke itself up, and it doesn't exist anymore.

But most of the members are still on the streets, all over the United States, still ripping people off. There's nothing to stop them.

8

Oddballs

PSYCHIATRISTS DON'T want to go to heaven; they all want to go to Beverly Hills. It's a shrink's paradise. The people here take to analysis the way winos in downtown LA take to muscatel, and with about the same results; the only difference is the price. Two business blocks in Beverly Hills—the 400 blocks of North Bedford and North Roxbury—contain more psychiatric couches than any other two blocks on earth.

So it was only Vegas odds that when the White House "plumbers" got their orders to break into the office of Daniel Ellsberg's psychiatrist, that office would be on Bedford or Roxbury. It's Suite 212 at 450 North Bedford.

Dr. Lewis Fielding phoned the police to report the break-in at eleven fifty the night of September 4, 1971; it was a Saturday night, and he had just heard about it from the janitor who discovered it, Efrain Martinez.

The date is important. In 1971 nobody outside the White House knew about the plumbers, almost nobody but the plumbers knew that Dr. Fielding had treated the guy who had leaked the Pentagon Papers to the press, and just about the only people who had ever heard of Watergate were the people who lived there.

125

So it looked like a routine minor case. Except that along the line it developed a few queer angles, some of which have never been explained.

It also got me sued for $2,000,000.

The guys who did it broke a window in the ground-floor office of Dr. Ashley Lipshutz to get into the building. They walked upstairs, pried part of the molding off Dr. Fielding's door, shimmed the lock open and just strolled in. Nothing was taken, but a little bottle of pain pills was opened and scattered across Dr. Fielding's desk. So it looked like a hype job where the guy didn't find what he wanted. Routine break and entry.

But it kept bothering me. When something doesn't fit, it usually means you've got the wrong answer. And in this case several things didn't fit.

For one thing, the blue suitcase. Clint Brickley, the uniformed officer who made the crime report investigation that Saturday night, heard about the suitcase from the janitor Martinez. He said two guys in mailmen's uniforms showed up about eleven o'clock the night before, Friday, when Martinez and his wife were cleaning up the place. The guys wanted to leave a blue suitcase in the office. Martinez and his wife said okay, and the guys left.

The next night, when Martinez discovered the break-in, the blue suitcase was gone. And nobody in Dr. Fielding's office knew anything about it; nobody had even been in the office because it was Saturday.

Another funny thing, Martinez told Clint the two guys spoke Cuban Spanish. We don't have too many Cubans in Beverly Hills, and a Cuban who is also a mailman is one hell of a rare bird. Seeing two of them at once, at eleven o'clock at night, is like sighting a flock of pterodactyls.

The business with the filing cabinets didn't make sense either. They were scratched and dented, like somebody had pried them open with a screwdriver. Clint figured they had been ransacked because some of the papers were piled around carelessly on top of the cabinets. But what would a hype want with a bunch of papers?

On top of all this the guys didn't touch anything in Dr. Lipshutz's place, and they didn't try to break into any other offices, which makes it look like Fielding was the only target.

"None of this fits the hype job theory," I said to Captain Rutherford about a week later.

"Why let it bother you?" Rutherford said. "Nothing was stolen, nobody else is worrying about it."

"Why won't Dr. Fielding talk to me?" I said.

Rutherford said, "How the hell should I know? Maybe he's busy."

I said, "He hasn't been busy all week. Every day I try to call him and every day it's the same story: 'Dr. Fielding is out of the office.' And he never calls me back. When does the son of a bitch do any work?"

Fielding took so long to call me back that I began to wonder if he thought I had some disease he could catch over the telephone. When he finally did call, in about a month, all he did was add another piece that didn't fit the puzzle. He was very upset when I asked about his files being ransacked.

"That's not true!" he said. "Nothing was taken, and nothing was disturbed!"

"Nothing?" I said.

"Nothing!" he said. He was practically shouting.

I said, "What about those marks on your filing cabinets, Doctor, and all your papers scattered around on top?"

And he said, "That's the way I keep them! Now look here, Mr. Franklin, I don't know why the police should be interested in this anyway, and I prefer that you don't contact me any further."

About all I could say was, "If that's what you want, okay, Doc." He was the victim, not the criminal, and it was not my job to hassle victims.

It was about this same time that I closed the case anyway

because we busted a guy named Finis Frankler on a two-bit theft, and he copped out to the Fielding break-in. He was lying, but we didn't know it at the time. What happened was that Frankler sneaked into the office of the Elizabeth Arden Salon on Wilshire at Roxbury and stole $22 out of the purse of the manager, Mrs. Lillian Mac-Millan. She had him arrested on the spot.

Frankler tried to con me into going easy on him by copping out to a whole bunch of little crimes. But this son of a bitch had the longest rap sheet I ever saw—seventy-eight arrests in thirty years of crime—and no way was I going to let him off easy.

"It's only petty theft," he said, "because it's under two hundred dollars."

"Bullshit, Frankler," I said. "I don't care if it's only a penny, you went in there with the intent to steal, and that makes it a felony."

"Look, Franklin," he said, "if my parole officer won't violate me, and if you'll just file for petty theft, I'll help you clear the books of the stuff I did."

I said, "Frankler, I won't do one goddamned thing to help you stay on the street."

He cooperated anyway, hoping I'd return the favor. And West LA Division of LAPD was able to clear sixteen jobs that he committed, jobs pretty much like the Elizabeth Arden job; all the victims ID'd his picture. And one of mine that he confessed was the Fielding break-in, so I just closed the case. I didn't check it any further.

My mistake.

We took the guy into Superior Court for felony burglary in the Elizabeth Arden case, we convicted him, and we sent him to prison. When he found out that I wasn't falling for his con, he got mad and filed a $200,000 damage suit against me and Mrs. MacMillan. It went nowhere; it was dismissed.

But that was only the beginning.

A year and a half later it came out at the Pentagon Papers trial of Daniel Ellsberg and Anthony Russo that it was the White House "plumbers" who broke into Dr. Fielding's office. The news guys came around asking questions, and Lieutenant Ed Greene looked it up in our records and gave out that we closed the case with the arrest of Finis Frankler, which was true.

Frankler, who by now had been in prison, out again, and was back in Folsom for another parole violation, started screaming that he couldn't have committed the break-in because he was in LA County Jail at the time, which also turned out to be true. I never got that far in my investigation because we couldn't prosecute him on that case anyway; we didn't have any physical evidence to back up his confession. If you can't take it to the DA, there's no use wasting your time and taxpayers' money on it.

Next, Frankler filed a $2,000,000 lawsuit against me and everybody else he could think of, from President Richard M. Nixon through John Ehrlichman, Egil Krogh and G. Gordon Liddy down to Chief Cork and Bruce Campbell. Only this time he left out Mrs. MacMillan. It was kind of funny because the only way he ever got connected with the Fielding break-in publicly was when his own goddamned lie boomeranged on him.

With all the publicity tying the break-in to Watergate, Dr. Fielding was suddenly famous. He was the Watergate star for a day, and everybody wanted to talk to him, which he enjoyed about as much as a CIA agent enjoys having his cover blown.

But he did file a sworn affidavit in the Ellsberg trial, and it was a whole different story from the one he told me. He said the locks on his file cabinets were bent out of shape and his papers were "thoroughly rummaged" and left in "considerable disarray."

Either he lied to me in 1971, or he lied to United States District Judge Matt Byrne in 1973. And either way I wanted to talk to him about it.

As usual, he didn't call back, but one day he complained to the police that suspicious people were hanging around outside his office building. I cruised by, and the suspicious people were an NBC film crew shooting their story in the street because Dr. Fielding wouldn't let them into his office. I didn't even slow down.

But after the suspicious characters had packed up their camera gear and disappeared back toward beautiful downtown Burbank, I parked and walked up to Suite 212. The receptionist said the doctor wasn't in, which was another lie because I could see through the half-open door into his private office and he was in there, wearing a zip-up jacket and a little skinny-brim hat like Frank Sinatra used to wear. He looked like a guy heading out for a fishing trip.

I just breezed on in for a little chat.

"Dr. Fielding," I said, "I can't understand it. After the break-in here you told me your files had not been pried open and your papers had not been tampered with. Now you're telling the federal court that, yes, you were the victim of a burglary and that they did pry into your files. Which is it?"

He said, "I can't understand why you are so concerned about this." He acted very nervous.

"Doc," I said, "I'm paid to be concerned. You pay me."

"Well," he said, "I have nothing to say to you."

"No kidding?" I said.

And he said, "Nothing whatsoever."

It was time to lay off, and that was what I did.

My guess now is Dr. Fielding lied to me in 1971, trying to cover up for some of the weird people he treated. If he had admitted to me that his files had been ransacked, I could come right back with: "Which files, Dr. Fielding?" Then he would have to tell me something, and anything he'd say could have burned some patient.

Anyway, I had a good reason to lay off now. Joe Busch, the district attorney of LA County, was having a big hassle with the federal people out of Washington, accusing the FBI of interfering with his own grand jury investigation of the break-in. I wasn't anxious to become a third party in that squabble; too many people were already investigating.

Busch was running the show in person when I was called to testify before the grand jury. And after I told all about Finis Frankler, Busch said, "When you arrest somebody like that, is it routine for you to take other crime reports that look similar and run them by him to see if you can clear up another case?"

He knew the answer, of course; he just wanted to get it on the record.

So I said, "It certainly is."

"Well," he said, "when Mr. Frankler admitted that he had been in that office, why didn't you file a case?"

I said, "Because I had no physical evidence to back up what he said."

Now Busch said, "Do you have any knowledge how many times Mr. Frankler has been arrested in his adult life?"

"Yes, sir," I said. "Since 1942 he has been arrested seventy-eight times."

And he said, "And *this* man is suing *you* for defamation of character?"

With that the whole grand jury completely broke up laughing.

But I hope I never get another case where the victim is a psychiatrist. They're crazy.

9

My Favorite Snitch

GOVERNMENT SPENDS millions of dollars every year trying to catch criminals with technology, but you might as well try to catch them with chicken soup. All of that *Mission: Impossible* stuff works great on TV, but in real police practice crimes are not solved in the laboratory or the computer; they're solved in the street.

Which is why I spend most of my time there. Police work is a people business, and the most important people a cop knows are his snitches because most crimes are solved on snitch information. I use more snitches and I spend more snitch money than all the other thirteen Beverly Hills detectives combined, and that's how I get results.

When darkness descends on Beverly Hills, so do the blacks. The town is a target. Which was why my favorite snitch, Len Swinger, happens to be black; Len must have tipped me to more than 100 jobs. Len is fifty-five now, and he has spent more than half of his life in prison. His father is about eighty-five, and he has spent more than half of that time in prison. Len has a son about twenty-eight who is doing life for murdering a cop. The whole family never did one honest thing, not once; they are all hypes, and all their

133

friends are hypes and thieves. If incompetence was a crime, they'd be locked up for good because they aren't even competent criminals.

The way I got acquainted with Len, one night I saw this old guy cruising around late, crossing and recrossing Olympic Boulevard, so I pulled him over and started asking questions. He was so foolish he told me he had to meet some guys; but he couldn't say exactly where, and it was two o'clock in the morning, and this didn't make sense. So I pressed him, and pretty soon he admitted that the guys he was supposed to meet were cleaning out an office building a couple of blocks away. This was my introduction to Old Man Swinger.

I got help, and we went to stake the place. Outside, in the back by the big trash bins, was a stack of office machines. Their MO was to stack the stuff like that, and after a while the old man would drive up, they'd pop the trunk lid and put the stuff away, and they'd split.

We waited awhile, and Len Swinger and another guy, Benny Watson, came out, and we busted them.

They had no machines, but their fingerprints were all over the ones that were already stacked outside. That and the fact they were on the scene were the only evidence we had to connect them to the job, which meant that the way the courts think we'd do well to put Len and Benny in county jail for ninety days, and if we could get the old man for an illegal left turn, it'd be a miracle.

But Len Swinger didn't know that, and he had a particular reason to want to stay away from county jail.

"Man," he said to me, "there is a deputy down there I don't want no truck with."

"Why not?" I said.

Len said, "He don't like me none. Last time I was in there, in the holding tank, my lawyer come to see me, and he said something made this dude mad. When the lawyer's gone, he stuffs me into a barrel and kicks me down the stairs. No, sir, man, I don't want to go back down there."

"Well, Len," I said, "maybe I can fix it so you don't have to go back there."

I let him think about that for a day or so, sitting there in the jail in Beverly Hills, and then I told him, "I got it all fixed, Len. All you got to do is cop out to this job, and I can get you a year at the Sheriff's Wayside Honor Farm."

Len took that for the biggest favor anybody had got since Grant won the war for Lincoln. "The day I get out," he said, "I'm going to turn something for you."

Len served his time at the farm, and at two thirty in the afternoon of the day he got out he walked into my office in the Detective Bureau. "Man," he said, "I told you I would turn something for you, and I got it. We're going to hit a travel agency on Wilshire in Beverly Hills about three o'clock in the morning. You want it?"

I said, "Who set it up? Did you?"

"Me? No," he said. "I'm with this guy, and he says, 'Look, man, you're just out, and I'm just out, and we need bread, so let's go get some.' This dude has been in for seven years."

"Okay," I said, "but don't you go setting anything up and then telling me about it. That's like playing my agent; that's entrapment. But if somebody invites you or tells you, that's okay." All the time I knew Len I had to keep telling him that. He had a tendency to get overambitious.

We staked on the travel agency, and about three in the morning this old Chevrolet sedan came rolling down Wilshire real slow. Two guys in it, but it was dark and I couldn't make them. The Chevy went around the corner and pulled in behind the building.

Half an hour later a guy walked out to the street from behind the building. He looked up and down the street like he was worried; he disappeared inside again; then he came out and started to walk out of the area.

Two of the uniformed guys went after him, and I went back to the Chevy. The backseat was stacked full of color TV sets; the keys were in the ignition, so I opened the trunk and it was full of IBM machines. I tried the ignition, and the car wouldn't start; the battery was dead, the motor was dead, something was dead. Now I knew why the guy tried to walk away.

When I started back out to the street, there was a whistle. I found Len crouched down behind a tree. He whispered to me, "What do I do?"

I said, "Get the hell out of here, man!" And he split.

Then I went on down to where my guys were holding the other guy, a real big dude, and I said, "What happened to your car back there, fellow?"

"My car?" he said. "What do you mean, my car? I'm just waiting for a bus."

He had a long wait. It was his broken-down car, his prints were all over the stuff in the car, and he left prints all over the penthouse office he had busted into. That was enough connection to lock him up again. And that was the beginning of my long relationship with Len Swinger.

Len isn't really a bad guy. He has no education except what he got at home, which was all about stealing. Nothing else ever occurred to him as an occupation. That, and he can't stay off the dope, which makes stealing a necessity. My problem as a cop is that society and the courts won't take a realistic look at the Len Swingers of this world and realize that they are incurable criminals.

"Look," he'd say to me, "I go to prison for a year, and they dry me out. When I'm isolated, I can go without it. I get out, and I think I'm okay. Then I get around some of the other guys, we start rapping, I see them popping, and I get right back in it again."

"Okay, Len," I would say. "Here's what I want you to do. Anytime, day or night, that you feel like getting a fix, just give me a call, and I'll get together with you, and we'll have some coffee, and we'll talk for as long as it takes; but you keep off that stuff."

"Anytime?" he said. "You mean that?"

"Anytime," I said more than once. "I don't care if it's four

A. M. or whatever; just call me, and I'll get out of bed and meet you. You can reach me through the department anytime.''

After that he called me many times, and we'd meet, usually at a coffee shop at Wilshire and La Brea, and we'd drink coffee and rap for hours, and old Len would leave as happy as a baby bear in a honey pot.

Then a couple of days later I'd pick up a teletype where somebody got busted; I'd look at the description, car used, the name—which almost always was an AKA, or Also Known As, an alias—and I'd say to myself, "That's got to be old Len Swinger." I'd call the place, and it would be Len all right, and he'd want me to get him out.

"Len," I said so many times I felt like a parrot, "when you go out and get busted, you're on your own." I wouldn't do anything for him. But he never stayed in long because the courts don't put criminals away, not very often. He'd call me, and we'd be back in business.

Somehow almost everything connected with Len Swinger had a funny angle. Like the case of Peewee Olds, which Len tipped me to. Peewee was unemployed—he always had been—but he went to the races at Hollywood Park every night of the season, he placed big bets, and he was a big tipper and a big spender. His real occupation was receiving.

Len told me that Peewee was fencing thirty expensive evening gowns that had been boosted from the Roos-Atkins clothing store, and the stuff was in his car. So I dropped by Peewee's house in the Wilshire District, a big place with iron bars on all the windows and the front door, and I told him I was looking for furs. I wanted to look in the trunk of his car.

"Okay, go ahead and look," he said.

We went out to the garage, and he opened the trunk, and there were the evening gowns, with the double sales tags still attached, the tags that they tear half off before anything leaves the store legally.

"Oh, fuck!" Peewee said. "I forgot all about putting that

stuff in there!" These guys really do get that careless.

There was more stuff in the house, and I had enough evidence to put Peewee away for six months. But the interesting thing was that he didn't think much of my clothes.

"Why don't you let me fix you up with a nice suit?" he said. I'm busting him, and he still wants to do business; he is such a compulsive salesman. He kept at it all through the trial.

"Look, Franklin," he said at the arraignment, "did you notice the suit my lawyer is wearing?"

I had noticed. It looked like a $450 thread collection.

"He buys all his suits from me," Peewee said. "Has for years, ever since the first time he defended me, when he was a public defender wearing forty-nine-dollar suits from J. C. Penney. Now he *looks* like a defense attorney."

"Yeah, well, thanks," I said. "I'm just a cop."

"Hell, what's the difference?" he said. "I'm talking J. C. Penney prices for class merchandise, and I don't play no favorites on either side of the law. I got a very distinguished clientele." And he named a bunch of lawyers and a federal district court judge and two Superior Court judges who bought their suits from him and who also sent their wives to him to buy their fancy rags.

They all knew it was stolen, and they didn't give a damn. But I didn't buy; I could never feel comfortable wearing stolen clothing.

There is about as much honor among thieves as among lawyers, which Len Swinger demonstrated after we met one afternoon at a pool hall down on 103d Street in what the newspapers have called South Central LA ever since the Watts people got annoyed at having everything blamed on them.

Len introduced me around as a friend of his who really did good things for him, and right away this one guy, Leroy, was trying to unload some TV sets on me.

"No," I said, "I'm not dealing in no kind of TV sets. If you got some furs or suede or some jewelry, I'll talk to you. But I'm not interested in TVs."

I couldn't discourage him. "I got some real stuff, see?" he said. "How about you come over to my house and see what I've got?"

Len said, "Let's go." He was interested even if I wasn't.

So we went over, and Leroy took us down to his basement, and it was like a discount house—color TV sets lined up by the dozen, all over the place. I ran my finger over one, and it had dust on it like it had been there from the day after Marconi.

I said, "Will they work?"

"Oh, they'll work," he said. "I guarantee it personally. None of them has ever even been turned on. They're brand-new."

"You know," I said, "I don't buy anything unless I know where it comes from. I got to know my sources."

He grinned and said, "Hey, man, you heard about the Watts riots?"

That son of a gun had been holding onto that stuff for years; he was afraid to let even one set go out. But now he was getting anxious about unloading them. He said, "Hey, you take everything I got here, I'll take twenty-five dollars per item. For everything."

I backed off. I said, "I don't like to have bulky stuff like that; it's too hot moving it around."

Two months later I went down to Len's place, and he had a couple of new TV sets. I said, "Hey, Len, where do you get the money to buy this kind of stuff?"

"No money," Len said.

I said, "Where do you get them?"

And he said, "You remember Leroy's basement that we went into?" That was why he was so interested in going with Leroy in the first place, so he could go back and rip him off.

Another travel agency job Len tipped me to didn't come

off because this time Len got sandbagged. He and two other guys were supposed to hit this place on Olympic, and I got four guys, and we staked on it all night. No action, nobody showed up.

The next morning I got a phone call from Len. He was in Pomona.

"You know why we didn't show up there?" he said.

I said, "What happened?"

"One of the guys talked us into coming out here instead to hit a DMV office," Len said. "And the cops was waiting for us. I'm in jail."

"Well," I said, "that's too bad. You're out of my jurisdiction."

Len said, "That son of a bitch set us up! I'm going to kill him!"

"Hey, Len," I said, "knock it off! What were you doing for me? You were bringing him to me, remember?"

"Yeah," he said, "but I'm going to get that motherfucking nigger!"

He did, too. He got another year at Wayside Honor Farm, courtesy of Pomona police. He was out in nine months with good behavior, and the same day he came into the Detective Bureau, just like before.

"That son of a bitch wants me to go on a job with him again," Len said. "You want him?"

I said, "I'll take him."

This time nobody got sidetracked, and we busted two guys pulling an office machine burglary on South Robertson.

But when we went to preliminary before Judge Zeller, a very typical thing happened: The defense attorney wanted to know the name of my informant, and the judge ordered me to spill it. The court and the defense didn't give a goddamn if the guy got his head blown off the next night, which is exactly what would happen to Len Swinger if his family and friends ever found out what he had done for me.

So I said, "Okay, his name is Willie."

Let them try and find Willie. There are 50,000 Willies in South Central LA, and 50,000 Leroys. Everybody knows somebody named Willie.

And generally that's all I want to know about a snitch, his street name. Before I'd burn a snitch, I'd throw the case. If I didn't, I'd never get anything again anyway.

When I needed money for a snitch, the chief had to get it from a special slush fund set up for this purpose and clear it with the city manager, George Morgan, and if you handed out very much, somebody upstairs got concerned and started asking questions. One time I needed money to bail a snitch out of county jail, and Morgan wanted to know, "Who the hell is he giving money to now?"

Chief Cork said, "I don't know."

"Well, now, wait a minute!" Morgan said. "We can't just be handing out money with no accounting of who it's for or what it's for."

"I'll tell you what," Cork said. "I don't want to know. Because if tomorrow this guy gets knocked off, I don't want them ordering me into court and asking did I know about this and did I know who the guy was. Now if you want, I'll have Franklin give you the name, and *you* can go to court if the guy gets killed. But I don't want to know."

Morgan backed off, and they handed me the money.

Len Swinger is always unpredictable because he is a hype; he never thinks anything through. Neither do his friends, like Benny Watson. Benny is a big guy about six feet four, 240 pounds and all man, but he got into drugs and got busted for murder in the army. He has been in trouble ever since; he has had about seventy busts since 1942.

I got word, not from Len but from another snitch, that it was Benny who had pulled a store burglary on my list of unsolved Beverly Hills cases, and now he was living in a crummy hotel on Sixth Street, just west of downtown LA.

Roger Bedford and I went down and knocked on his door, and he said, "Yeah, who is it?"

"Hey," I said, "it's Willie."

That always works. He opened the door, and we busted in and ripped the place apart. Under the mattress I found a hype kit. I took it out, laid it on the floor and stomped it.

And that great big guy broke down and cried like a woman. "Please!" he said. "You can do anything in the world to me, but please don't bust my hype kit, they're too hard to come by."

"Benny," I said, "it's already busted, so stop crying. Maybe you won't need it for a while anyway."

Three days after I booked him, he bailed out and called me up. "Hey, Franklin," he said, "did you tow my car in?"

I said, "No, why?"

"It was sitting in front of the hotel there when you busted me. A black Lincoln Continental."

"I didn't tow your car in," I said. "The car had nothing to do with the arrest."

"Well," he said, "it's gone. What should I do?"

I said, "Benny, if I were you, I'd go report it stolen."

He called up LAPD Rampart Division and reported the car stolen. Then a little later Len Swinger drove up to the hotel in Benny's car; it wasn't stolen. They rapped a little and decided to go pull a heist at Wilson's House of Suede. And a little after that they were driving down Wilshire Boulevard, and LAPD pulled them over for stolen car. Benny had forgotten to call and cancel the stolen car report. And in the trunk was all the leather and suede from Wilson's House of Suede, so those two clowns got busted for that too.

One thing with a snitch: You've got to stay right on him. I would tell Len, "I don't care if you don't have any information for me, I want to hear from you every two or three days. And don't ever move from one place to another without letting me know. If I go to your pad and you've moved away, it bothers me. I want to know where you are and what's going on, what jobs you're pulling."

"Me?" he said. "I'm not pulling jobs anymore."

"Look," I said, "you couldn't go three days without pulling a job, and I know it, so don't try to tell me any different. Just tell me what you're doing."

A guy like Len ought to be put away as a habitual criminal, but the system doesn't work that way. So if he's going to be forced to stay on the street, I figure I might as well take advantage of what the courts are forcing on me. But you let a guy like that stay away from you for a week, he gets lost. Len was always getting lost, and I would have to go look for him.

One time that I couldn't locate him I got his parole officer, Sonny Dallenbach, into the act. He located Len and brought him into the courthouse in Beverly Hills, and we met in the corridor outside Division 1. There were a lot of people wandering around, attorneys and defendants and everybody else, so we had a good audience for the act.

All of a sudden Sonny turned on Len and he said, "Len Swinger, you no-good black son of a bitch, I hate your goddamned guts! I hate your mother, I hate your father, I hate your son, I hate your whole damned family! Every one of you are thieves!"

And Sonny turned to me and said, "Franklin, do you want me to violate the son of a bitch and throw him back into prison?"

I said, "Well, Sonny, I haven't made up my mind yet. But the way he's backing off and reneging on me, I don't know whether he can do me any good. Maybe he should go back to prison."

That kind of shook Len up. He was reacting like he was mad, which is only his way of doing business; he was really scared. Sonny read him off for maybe another five minutes.

Finally, he said, "Okay, Len, I'm going to leave you on the street for now, but you black motherfucking son of a bitch, if Franklin calls me and tells me you've backed off, you've failed to fulfill just one promise to him, I'll denut you, you son of a bitch!"

Old Len got religion for a good month after that, but then he backslid, and I was looking for him again.

This time I found him in a second-floor apartment on La Salle Avenue, down near the University of Southern California. I tapped on the door, no answer. You could tell, by the looks of it, that door had been kicked in many times; it was that kind of place. But first I tried to get the landlady to let me in.

"They ain't in there," she said.

"Aw, come on," I said, "I know they're in there."

"They ain't there."

"Give me a key, and I'll go in and see."

"I ain't giving you no key."

I said, "Okay, then you'll have to build a new door again."

Just a little light kick was all it took, and inside was Len with Bugs Parkane, who used to be a very famous drummer with all the big jazz bands until the dope got him. They must have had the heat turned up to a hundred and forty; hypes get cold sometimes, and when they do, they like it hot enough to cook steel bearings.

Bugs was sitting on a bed, far out, probably dreaming of the good old days with Basie and Ellington and Goodman. Len was leaning over the windowsill with the biggest screwdriver I ever saw in my life—big enough to pry open Fort Knox—and he was prying at the window with it, practicing.

"Len," I said, "what the hell are you doing with that screwdriver?"

He said, "Me? I'm just showing Bugs."

"What are you showing Bugs?"

"Just showing Bugs something." He wouldn't tell me what he was showing Bugs.

So I said, "You know, Len, the cops can break in here any time, and if you got that screwdriver, it's like your fingerprints. They can make it to a dozen different jobs you've been on."

He never did learn his lesson. Most times he'd get arrested it would be because he went on a job without gloves and got made on his prints. After all the times he'd been caught, Len Swinger always thought he'd never get caught again, he thought he could always con anybody, and he always had an answer. The answer might not make sense to anybody else, but it sounded good to him.

Like another time he got lost and I went looking for him with Roger Bedford down at Old Man Swinger's house. We knocked on the door, and I heard the old man yell, "Yeah, who is it?"

So I just pushed the door open easy and went right on in. We could hear them upstairs, so we went up and found the old man, Bugs Parkane, Benny Watson and a couple of other guys sitting around.

I said, "Mr. Swinger, where's Len?"

He said, "Mr. Franklin, I don't know." When Old Man Swinger and I got together, for some reason we talked very formal. "Len was around here two, three days ago," he said, "but he just up and walked out of here. I haven't seen him for two, three days."

Neither had anybody else. But they all seemed to be paying too much attention to a little low door, so I walked over and opened the door.

Behind it was a little, cramped closet under the eaves of the house, and crouched in there in the dark, holding his hand over his pipe to keep the smoke from coming out, was Len Swinger.

"Oh, hello there," he said, looking up at me like he was really surprised. "What are you doing here, Lynn?"

I said, "Len, I came down here looking for you."

"Hey, man!" he said. "I was just going to call you. I was just looking for a phone to call you."

And to prove it he held out his hand, showing me a dime in his palm.

It's pretty hard to hate a guy like that.

10

A Touch of Vice

WE ALMOST never work prostitutes in Beverly Hills; it's a waste of time. As long as the customer gets what he pays for, we don't get involved.

But when the girls start ripping off their tricks, the city fathers get interested because it is bad for business; it gives Beverly Hills a bad reputation. And then of course the police department has to get interested.

The way the prostitute usually works it, she takes some businessman from out of town up to his hotel room and gives him a fast job; then she says, "Hey, honey, you go in and take a shower, and when you come out, I'll really turn you on."

So the old guy goes into the shower, and when he comes out, eager again, the girl is gone, and so are his money, his credit cards, his traveler's checks, his jewelry and anything else that's loose. He wouldn't know the girl from Eve; about the only thing he remembers is the shape of her crotch, which is not a very reliable means of identification.

Whether we were working vice or not, I always got acquainted with all the prostitutes I could because they were an amazing source of information. A trick will open up and tell a whore things he would never tell his wife or even his lawyer, and if you are friendly, the girl would pass it all on.

One that I turned into a snitch was Lola Brown, a cute little brunette I picked up at the bar in the Luau Restaurant one night when Joe Langer and I were working vice because of the rip-offs. Lola had a girlfriend, and they agreed to go with us to a room I had rented in the Beverly Rodeo Hyatt House, which is just across the street and down a block from the Luau.

Lola said, "I'll sell you my pantyhose for fifty bucks."

"Okay," I said, "Let's go!"

I already had my room key, but I had never been up to the room, so when we got off the elevator, I didn't know which way to turn.

"Oh, hell!" I said. "We must have come up on the wrong elevator. I don't know where my room is."

Lola said, "What number is it?"

I looked at the key and said, "Four oh six."

And she said, "I know where it is, just follow me." She probably knows every hotel bed in Beverly Hills.

We got in the room, and both girls started stripping faster than I could close the door. Lola had a little jumpsuit on, which she ripped off, and she dropped her pantyhose and held them out to me.

"All right," she said, standing there in panties and bra, "how about my fifty bucks and we'll get down to business?"

Joe was stalling for time, and the other girl was already lying naked on one of the beds, waiting for him, but now she looked up at me and went big-eyed as I reached for my hip pocket.

I pulled out the badge, and I said, "You know, honey, I hate to do this, but you're under arrest."

Lola looked at the badge, and all she said was, "Oh, shit!" She grabbed her car keys out of her purse and let me have it across the cheek. I still have the scar; it's the only one I picked up in twenty years of police work.

After I cooled her down and did the constitutional rights routine, Lola said, "You can't arrest me. All I did was offer to sell you my pantyhose."

"Who told you that?" I said.

"My attorney told me that," she said. "There's nothing against the law in selling clothes, and if something happens later, it's not prostitution."

"Who's your attorney?"

"Larry Warren."

"He told you to do this pantyhose bit?"

"Hell," she said, "you don't think I thought that up by myself?"

"Well," I said, "put the jumpsuit back on. I'm keeping the pantyhose as evidence, and we'll see."

Larry Warren practically has a corner on the legal business for prostitutes, pimps and fags, and this is why: He advises them *before* they commit the crime, not just after.

The American Bar Association says lawyers are not supposed to help or tolerate the "commission of an unlawful act," and they are supposed to let the court know anything that would protect the victims of crime. That's called Formal Opinion Number 155. Larry Warren breaks that rule of his profession almost every day, and his brother lawyers and the courts salute him because he is getting rich breaking their rules.

Lola turned snitch for me because I got her probation instead of jail. She would have gotten only maybe thirty days, but the cells in county jail don't have the class of the hotel rooms she is accustomed to.

The first case she turned for me I never even got inside a courtroom; but I had the satisfaction of shafting Larry Warren, and that was worth it. What happened was a booster mob hit Beverly Hills, and they were practically cleaning the whole town out of expensive leather and suede clothing. Every store got hit, and hard.

Stores won't admit it, but most of them won't prosecute ordinary shoplifting, especially if they get their merchandise back. The hassle in the courts isn't worth the trouble, even when they get a conviction.

But boosting is different. Boosting compared to shoplifting is like a world war compared to an alley fight; too much money is involved to just forget it. Boosters operate in gangs that are highly trained and organized to work a place over. Two or three girls go into a store wearing booster bags or booster girdles, and half an hour later they'll walk out with thousands of dollars' worth of furs or leather or jewelry or whatever their specialty is.

It's nearly always girls because they can hide more stuff under their clothes than men, especially with the long floppy dresses they wear these days. But the girls all take orders from men who run the gangs; it's the same arrangement as prostitutes and pimps, and sometimes booster girls are whores, too, and almost always they are hypes. That's why a girl goes into boosting, to pay for her habit.

We had no leads on the leather boosters until Lola picked up some information from a trick who had bought a hot leather jacket down in the Echo Park neighborhood in LA from some guy and a girl named Delilah, and Delilah had let drop that she came from Columbus, Ohio. And they had a house full of leather.

I checked Columbus, and they had busted a Delilah Dancey a couple of years before for boosting, along with two other gals and three guys. They hadn't heard of any of them for a while.

So Campbell and I went to the house in Echo Park, and a girl answered the door.

I said, "Is Delilah here?"

Delilah was inside, and she heard me and yelled out, "Yeah, I'm here. Come on in."

She thought I was somebody she knew, so I walked in with a gold-plated invitation, and here was my booster team, three guys and three gals, and enough leather lying around to recoat the biggest herd of cattle in Texas. The stuff was stacked all over the place, plus there were a dozen big booster bags all filled, tagged, ready to ship and addressed to Columbus, Ohio.

There wasn't a label in anything; it all came from nowhere. People who make up expensive fur pieces that sell for $5,000 or $10,000 stamp their own little code on the inside leather under the lining, so boosters will pass up that stuff. But this stuff was not that expensive, it had no code stamps, and all they did was rip out the labels.

"Who gave you the right to confiscate all that stuff and bring it in?" said Bob Sills, the deputy DA who handled the case.

I said, "It's stolen property, Bob."

He said, "Who told you?"

"Experience," I said. "How many suede jackets you got in your closet with every label and ID ripped out?"

"That's no proof," he said.

And I said, "The hell it isn't! If I recover a hundred suede and leather coats, all new, and every damned label is ripped out, that's proof! When you buy a leather jacket you buy the label too, you want people to see it—I. Magnin, Saks, Bullock's, Wilson's House of Suede, whatever. No labels *is* proof!"

But I couldn't get anybody to ID the stuff. I had manufacturers and dealers come in from all over, and they'd say, "Well, that looks like our merchandise, but without the label there is no way I could swear to it."

And I couldn't get Bob Sills to file a case. It's bad enough dealing with crooks, it's worse dealing with lawyers and judges, but real frustration is when you can't get your DA to file your case and at least give you a try at convicting the people you busted.

"You had no right to open up any of those booster bags ready for shipment," Bob said.

I said, "Then why do you call them booster bags?"

"Dammit, Franklin," he said, "you irritate the hell out of me. I pick up your language, that's why."

And I said, "Bob, I *knew* I was dealing with a booster gang. That's what gave me the right to open those bags or look for evidence any place in that house. I had legal reason to believe that the stuff in those bags was boosted merchandise."

He wouldn't go for it. He kicked the whole case out and turned everybody loose. He wouldn't even file grand theft auto in regard to the stolen car parked outside their pad, a car that they had stolen in Ohio and driven to LA.

"Call the FBI," Bob said. "Maybe they'll prosecute them."

I said, "Okay, you son of a bitch, maybe someday you'll be a good DA, but you sure as hell have got a way to go. The only thing you know how to write is a rejection." And I started to walk out.

We were in his office, which was on the fourth floor of the court building in Beverly Hills, and there was a little ledge outside the window in the hall. Bob got up and started to follow me out.

"Franklin," he said, "you don't understand."

I turned to face him, and I said, "Look, Bob, don't follow me out this goddamned door, because if you do, I'm going to throw you off that ledge out there."

He didn't follow me because it was four floors down to solid concrete and he knew I meant it, I was that mad. He issued an order for all the deputy DAs in Beverly Hills that any case of mine had to go directly to him. That order stood for two years. Later he got transferred to Santa Monica, in the Superior Court jurisdiction, and he grew up and got tough. He handled my big Tiffany robbery case, by which time he had turned into a fighting son of a gun and we became good friends. Now I'm glad I didn't throw him off that ledge.

A couple of days after the booster gang went free Larry Warren called me. He was their lawyer.

"Franklin," he said, "I want to know when my clients can come down and claim their property," meaning all the leather I had confiscated.

I said, "Larry! Goddamn, I'm glad you called me. I've made almost all of that stuff now, but don't you tell them that. As they come down and claim the stuff, I'll rebook them for receiving stolen property. So you just send them on down. And, Larry?"

"Yeah?" he said, pretty sour.

"It's a pleasure to do business with you," I said. "I appreciate your cooperation, Larry."

Of course, they never came for the stuff. Larry warned them not to. I hadn't really made one piece of that leather, but Larry swallowed my line. We kept the stuff in the warehouse for a year; then the city sold it at auction for $10,000. It was worth a lot more, but you couldn't get the price without the labels. Anyway, it was ten Gs that I figured came out of Larry Warren's hide, so I bought Lola Brown a couple of drinks and thanked her for the pleasure.

Her information also solved the murder of Lionel Reed, a finance company vice-president who picked up a black prostitute in Beverly Hills one night and turned up the next morning robbed, shot dead and dumped out in the Hollywood Hills. LAPD Homicide and the FBI came to me with it because of the prostitute angle and they knew I had a thing going with Lola. So I talked to her.

"Yeah," she said, "I know what probably happened. I used to be Lionel's steady date until he started playing around with this black girl, through her pimp. It was weird, a threesome like that; I think Lionel got kind of kinky. I hear they took him over to an eight-dollar-a-night fleabag in Hollywood, and when he didn't have any money, they killed him and dumped him out in the Hollywood Hills."

I said, "What do you mean, no money?"

"They thought he had money, but he didn't. He never did. He would meet me every week, every Thursday night, and he always brought exactly fifty-five dollars with him. Fifty for me and five for he and I to have a drink. Then we'd have sex, and I'd go home. And these people thought because he was with that finance company that he had a lot of money."

Lola gave us the name of the pimp, Marvin Wile, we put out a pickup, and the next week San Francisco grabbed him. He had one of Lionel Reed's credit cards on him, and LAPD brought him back and convicted the son of a bitch of murder.

One thing that's consistent about pimps and prostitutes: Anytime they get busted, they'll demand a public defender.

To get a public defender, you're supposed to be without funds, you're legally indigent. That's the law. But the curb slots around the Beverly Hills Municipal Court look like the parking lot at Hillcrest Country Club, with all the Pimp Specials—the big Cadillacs and Continentals that are owned by pimps who are upstairs being defended by public defenders. The public defender's office, which is supposed to check out the finances of these people, doesn't want to know that they own $12,000 cars.

The filthiest pimp I ever knew had a male prostitute ring that he ran for nine years out of a duplex apartment on Fountain Avenue in West Hollywood. We only got onto it when there was some mixup in dates and two of his young studs came to service a Beverly Hills dentist at almost the same time. Jealousy took charge.

One of the boys, Jerome Wilkie, went to the dentist's apartment on Olympic Boulevard, and walked in and found

Dr. Lannan Shaw already in bed enjoying the attentions of Wilkie's competitor, Maxwell Phillips.

Wilkie and Shaw were old bedmates, so maybe it was love and maybe it was the money, but Wilkie pulled out a little over-and-under .22 caliber derringer and took a shot at Phillips. Lucky for both of them, the derringer is a lady's gun that's about as accurate as a Frisbie; the bullet just made a hole in the wall behind the bed.

But it woke up a neighbor, who called the department; we surrounded the apartment building and arrested Wilkie as he was walking out. The damned fool had the derringer in his right back pocket, still cocked and with a live round in the second barrel; at that range if he had wiggled his ass, his own gun would have shot it off.

Wilkie told us the "he-madame" was a guy named Robert Bolton. Wilkie had introduced maybe fifteen young guys to him, and Bolton made them strip and inspected their "meat," and if they had enough, he put them to work.

Bolton's front was a massage business, but if anybody called and dropped a code number, "four thirteen," that meant he didn't want a rubdown, he wanted fag sex.

That night I checked into the Beverly Hilton Hotel under the name of Gary Rollins, from Miami Beach. I called Bolton's number and when he answered, I said, "Lee recommended that I call you. Do you remember Lee?"

"Oh, sure," he said. I didn't know any Lee, and he didn't know Lee or wouldn't remember, but that wasn't important. It was like Willie or Leroy; only this was white.

"Does four thirteen mean anything?" I said.

"Yes, of course," he said. "Four thirteen. What would you like?"

I said, "Well, I'm just in from Florida. I'm at the Beverly Hilton. Can you send somebody over to my room?"

And he said, "In half an hour. I have a stable of young boys well experienced in showing you a good time and satisfying your every sexual desire."

Jackpot!

I said, "How much is it?"

He said, "The price is twenty-five dollars for the first hour and twenty dollars each for any additional hours."

"Okay," I said. And I ordered up a date, and I gave Bolton my room number and my phony name, Gary Rollins.

Half an hour later a guy knocked on the door and introduced himself as Don. I told him to come in and make himself comfortable while I ordered some drinks.

"What's the price?" I said.

He gave me the same price that was quoted on the telephone.

I said, "What do I get for that?"

"Whatever you want," he said. "You can have a fuck in the ass, or I'll give you a head job." And he took off his clothes and got onto the bed naked, with a big erection.

I opened the door, Bruce Campbell and Wayne Rutherford popped into the room, and we busted the guy. His real name turned out to be Don Rissler, and he was a part-time actor.

"Okay, Don," I told him, "I'm going to call Bolton again, and I want you to talk to him. I want you to tell him we're good people, we're good pay, and we're having a party over here, and we need another boy."

Don did like he was told, and in a little while there was another knock on the door. It was Maxwell Phillips, and he recognized me right away from the Wilkie bust a couple of nights before. He tried to split, but I caught him at the elevator. Now we had two in the bag.

They told us Bolton's operation went as far as Hawaii, where he had a recruiter who told young guys getting out of the military and heading back to the mainland to get in touch with Bolton and he'd give them part-time work. It was even a couple of Bolton's boys that went up to Ramon Novarro's house the night the old actor got killed.

That night Campbell and I kicked in the door of Bolton's place on Fountain Avenue. Nobody was there, but the place was loaded with disgusting photos of homosexuals going at each other, and he had a big trick book with the names of all his customers in it. Some of them were the biggest names in television and movies, international stars who are millionaires because they're good actors or they're good at jokes on television. My phony name was in the book too: "Gary Rollins, Miami Beach, Beverly Hilton," and the date and the times I had called, and the names of the boys he had sent me.

But we didn't get Bolton. He had spooked.

A couple of days later Larry Warren called me. He said, "Franklin, I hear that you are looking for a client of mine, Bob Bolton."

"Bolton?" I said. "Gee, it doesn't connect, Larry. I'm not looking for anybody by that name. But I'll ask around and see if anybody else is."

The Detective Bureau is just a big open room, with desks along each wall, and Larry knows it because he has been there many times. So I yelled around to the guys, and nobody had ever heard of Bob Bolton, and Larry Warren listened to all of this.

"Sorry, Larry," I said. "You sure you got the right jurisdiction?"

This reassured him, and he told Bolton that he could go home again. But meanwhile, we were getting a search warrant, and the next night we went back to Fountain Avenue and we busted Bolton and all his dirty books and pictures.

Larry Warren got continuance after continuance from Judge Armand Zeller, and finally Bolton got straight probation, not a day in jail. Larry won that one, from a judge who was an easier lay than Lola Brown.

Lola finally disappointed me. She got involved with a guy in Orange County, and they busted her down there for pigeon drop. I never thought Lola would stoop so low. She told them to call me, but when they did, I just said, "Put her away if you can." She got one to five and she's still in prison.

One problem with prostitution is that you can't ignore it

if somebody calls it to your attention, which is what happened when President Sukarno of Indonesia came through Beverly Hills on his way to Washington to con some federal money out of the government.

I was still in uniform then, and they put me on security. Sukarno and about thirty of his people stayed at the Beverly Hills Hotel, and I had a desk right at the elevator where anybody who wanted to visit them had to get off.

There were a lot of Secret Service guys running around the place, and one of them came over to me one night and said, "There's some girls coming up here, and I want you to know so you'll let them in."

"Girls?" I said.

"Prostitutes," he said.

And I said, "Now you shouldn't have told me that, because we have a law about it in Beverly Hills. I'll have to arrest them."

"Jesus Christ!" the guy said. "This is for President Sukarno himself and some of the others. It is all arranged."

I didn't want to create an international incident, so I said, "Look, friends are okay. But prostitutes, no."

And he said, "Okay, we'll send up some friends."

Pretty soon three girls walked out of the elevator, and one of them was Mabel Cunningham, a redheaded prostitute I know well around Beverly Hills. She gave me a funny look, and the girls started down the hall.

"Hold it," I said. "Wait a minute."

Mabel swung around and glared at me, thinking maybe she had been set up. She said, "What the hell is this, Lynn?"

I said, "Mabel, where are you going?"

And she said, "We're going to visit a *friend* of mine, President Sukarno." She breathed so heavy on that word "friend" that I worried about her health.

"Okay," I said, "if you're friends, you can go ahead."

They went on down the hall, and for the next couple of hours I could see down there where they were yo-yoing back and forth from President Sukarno's suite to somebody else's room across the hall and then back again. They were busier than a banjo player on Saturday night.

Finally, they came back to the elevator, all messed up and their hair wild, and Mabel was now all smiles.

"Boy, what a night!" she said.

I said, "I guess you made out all right."

And she said, "Lynn, I made enough to take off for months."

The way those Indonesians threw money around, that probably was prostitution's biggest night in the history of Beverly Hills. It was all American taxpayer money which the State Department gave those guys to enjoy their stay, and they would walk by me with huge wads in their hands and they didn't know a hundred-dollar bill from a dime—it was all the same to them. They went on to Washington and got a big American loan to keep the Communists from taking over their country, and then they went home, and Indonesia went Communist and stayed that way several years. Mabel and her girlfriends were the only people who got a good deal out of Sukarno.

Some cops never learn how to work vice, and one who doesn't is Johnny Burns, who is one of the department's forgery experts. Johnny can tell a phony signature on a check from a hundred yards blindfolded, but he can't tell a phony woman when he's in bed with her. He goes to extremes: First, he is too intellectual, and when he isn't, he lets his heart guide him.

In Beverly Hills we all did almost every job at one time or another, and one night Johnny wound up working vice with me and Bruce Campbell and Ed Zenter at the Chez Voltaire, which is the bar in the Beverly Rodeo Hyatt House. This is an intimate little place, which translates crowded, and there are always some interesting people in show business just sitting around and having a drink and talking.

So we were working and pretending not to know each

other, and in came a gal I knew well, Marcia Sansone, who was a wealthy middle-aged dyke but could be mistaken for a prostitute because she always wore flashy clothes with her big knockers hanging out, and her war paint was so thick she looked like she was made up by Forest Lawn. Marcia was married to a Chinese smuggler who got kicked out of the country years ago, and she wound up with a taste for thrills and the money to afford them. She loved young girls. She'd go up to a room with you, but only if you brought a young girl along, so you had a threesome. And she wouldn't charge you; she'd pay you.

Marcia threw me a smile and sat down at the bar next to Johnny Burns, and right away he started making a play for her. I thought, *Oh, goddammit, Johnny!* But I couldn't get a signal to him because Marcia was right there beside him.

Then another gal I knew came walking in, Hilda Long, a prostitute that I had busted, and she gave me a wave and sat down on the other side of Johnny. She knew Marcia, and they started talking across Johnny, and now he was making a play for both of them, and I knew damned well Johnny's cover was blown.

When the Chez closed at two o'clock in the morning, the three of them went out and got in Hilda's car, and they drove down to Lenny's Delicatessen for coffee and breakfast. We watched them go in, and then we went back to the station.

At four o'clock in the morning Johnny still hadn't come in. I radioed a beat unit to check, and sure enough, he was still in Lenny's, carrying on with those two gals, spending city money on a prostitute who had already made him for cop and a dyke he could never get anything on.

I stiffed in a phone call to Lenny's, got Johnny and said, "Get your ass out of there; dump those gals and right away."

Johnny said, "Oh, no, I'm starting to get somewhere with them. I'm working up to something."

"Johnny," I said, "Marcia's a dyke, and Hilda knows we were working the Chez, and she is not going to give you a toss tonight. She is probably not out for a guy tonight. They're just taking you for a ride on your expense money."

He objected some more, but after about $30 he gave up and came in. I called Hilda at her place, and she had just got in. I put Johnny on the phone and told her to give him the score. She did, and it really hurt his pride because he thought he had really conned them.

A couple of nights later we were working a bar in the Beverly Hilton, and Johnny picked up a little blond beauty, Mary Shore, and they went up to the room. The way we worked it then, one guy did the pickup and the other guy hid in the closet, listening so he could be a witness. Richard Rodriguez was in the closet.

The minute Mary got in the room she stripped off and jumped into bed. Johnny was taking his shirt off slow, stalling, trying to get her to quote a price because if it's free, it's not arrestable.

"Come *on!*" she said. "Get in bed!"

He said, "Hey, how much is this going to cost me?"

"Cost you?" she said. "What the hell are you talking about? Just get in bed, and let's fuck."

Johnny couldn't get Mary to name a price, and finally he began to realize that she was just out to play, she was not in the business.

"Look, honey, I'm sorry," he said, while Rodriguez in the closet was busting a gut trying to laugh without making any noise. "I'm a cop," Johnny said, "I'm working a vice detail."

"I don't give a goddamn what you are!" Mary said. "Get in bed with me. I want to fuck!"

"You don't understand," Johnny said. "I'm a vice cop; we're out to arrest people."

He couldn't convince her. "Arrest, my ass!" she said. "Just get into this bed, and let's get it on!"

It took awhile, but finally, he convinced her, and she got her clothes back on and went downstairs. I kidded Johnny about it later that night. "It wasn't very nice of you to let the lady go like that, all frustrated," I said.

"Jesus Christ!" Johnny said. "I wanted like hell to oblige her, but Richard was in the closet."

The night wasn't entirely wasted. Johnny made a date to meet Mary for breakfast, and he found out she was a wealthy gal just getting a divorce and she had a big house up in Coldwater Canyon. They got to be good friends, and ever since then Johnny spends a lot of time in Coldwater Canyon.

11

The Unreported Crime

ONE WHOLE summer in Beverly Hills we had a rapist who operated on a schedule as regular as the Wilshire bus, and we couldn't lay a finger on the guy. We piled up eleven unsolved cases at the rate of about one a week, which meant that he pulled a job practically every day all summer long because for every rape that's reported there are maybe ten more you don't hear about.

Older women will report a rape, but a lot of the younger ones won't; they screw around so much anyway that they don't think it's important. All our victims were older women; the youngest was fifty, and the oldest was seventy-eight.

This busy bastard was an afternoon man; he never raped in the morning. He would knock on a door, and when a woman answered, he would ask for her husband. If she was careless enough to say, "He's not here," the guy would force his way in and rape her. He was driving us crazy.

Finally, I found a suspect to fit the descriptions we were getting, a guy named John Stanley who had a football scholarship at UCLA and got kicked out and convicted for raping a coed. I put together a six-photo lineup and showed the pictures to three of my victims, and all three positively identified him.

One of the girls, an Oriental named Alma Tabori, pointed to the web between her thumb and forefinger on her right hand and said, "When you find him, you're going to find a big scar there. He was trying to choke me, and I bit him there. I bit the hell out of him."

The guy lived on Grape Street down in Willowbrook, which is Crip territory. The Crips are a black gang so vicious that they should be exterminated like vermin; the good black people down there are scared to death of them, and that part of town is more dangerous than Harlem ever was. There is a public housing project near there, Nickerson Gardens, where the people have to sleep on the floor while bullets fly through their rooms at night, and they can't leave an apartment for ten minutes or they'd come back and find it stripped clean of everything.

Sometimes in telling about crime, it sounds like all blacks are criminals, which they are not. Most of them are not. And I have had to deal with plenty of white criminals, like that whole Red Velvet Gang and the ski-mask bandits.

But most of our violent street crime is committed by blacks. When I spoke to the Chamber of Commerce, they wanted to know about that, so I just pulled out the files on the last fifty cases I had handled, and forty-nine were black and one was Mexican-American. Never mind the sociological reasons; this is the problem the police have to deal with, and this is why I had to chase down to South Central LA so many times.

One time I was talking about that with Eddie Dickson, a black guy in the department from Tennessee, and me being from Mississippi, we kidded around a lot. And I said something about, "More than eighty percent of the violent street crime in Beverly Hills is committed by blacks."

And Eddie said, "Lynn, when did you get to be such a goddamned liberal? You know damned well it's more than *ninety* percent."

So Ed Zenter and I went down and staked on John Stanley's house on Grape Street. We had told the Department to notify the sheriff's Firestone Division because that is their territory, and pretty soon their detective commander, Lieutenant Dewayne Primesburger, came on the radio.

"Jesus Christ!" he yelled. "Get the hell out of there, you guys! That's Crip turf, and they're sniping every white that comes down the street! Get out of there!"

We didn't want to make trouble for Primesburger, so we went back to Beverly Hills, we presented what we had to the DA, and we got a warrant for Stanley's arrest.

Then we went back to Primesburger, and we said, "Okay, we've got a warrant, we're going to go get the guy, and if you want to give us some help, that'll be fine." He gave us some backup units, and Zenter and I were to make the original contact.

Just as we approached the house, Stanley came running out like he was fired from a circus cannon. He jumped in his car and headed south on Grape Street. We went in pursuit. We were about a block behind, and suddenly a car backed out of a driveway and came to a dead stop crossways in the street right in front of us. The car was loaded with black guys staring at us; it was like the whole neighborhood was trying to help Stanley split, which maybe it was.

We went around them, up over the curb and through somebody's yard, cutting big ruts, but by the time we got back into the street Stanley had made a turn and got away. The black guys were still just sitting there, staring at us; they probably were Crips—those guys will challenge the cops any time they outnumber you.

We put out a call, and almost immediately a Firestone Division black deputy found Stanley in a Union gas station parking lot on Imperial Highway.

"I got him spotted," the deputy radioed. "I'm approaching him." He got out of his car, pulled his gun and yelled at Stanley, "I'm a police officer. Freeze!"

And Stanley did a crazy thing, the first of many crazy

things that happened in the next few minutes. He jumped
out of his car and ran straight at the deputy; he was coming
straight at that gun muzzle. The deputy had every right to
shoot him, but he decided to wrestle him instead. He
grabbed him, and he could feel a snub-nosed revolver in
Stanley's coat pocket.

Stanley broke loose and ran down Imperial. The whole
place was turning into a mob scene. Everybody was coming
out into the street to see the show, which is what they do in
that neighborhood when anything happens in the summertime; there must have been a thousand people milling all
over the street by the time we pulled up to join the chase.

Stanley hesitated and reached in his jacket like he was
going for the snub-nose, and that black deputy laid it down
on him and emptied his gun. But the guy was weaving and
dodging, and he wasn't hit. The lucky part was nobody else
in that crowd was hit either. A beauty shop took all the bullets; the holes were still in the wall last time I drove by.

Next move, Stanley started across Imperial, and he was
shucking his jacket with the snub-nose in the pocket,
which somebody in the crowd picked up. We never saw it
again.

Suddenly a white car with three white guys in it turned
the far corner and stopped. One guy rolled out, dropped
down and laid three shots on Stanley, which drove him
right back across the street into our arms.

The amazing thing was that thirteen shots were fired in
the middle of that mob scene, and nobody got scratched.
When the white guy started shooting, he was practically
shooting at us, and we were practically shooting at him,
with Stanley in the middle of the sandwich; it was as crazy
as the joke about the Italian firing squad which forms in a
circle.

The white guy got back in the white car, and they split,
and I said to Dewayne Primesburger, "Have you got that
unit working?"

"No," he said, "they're not ours. That's the one we call the phantom car."

"Well, who the hell can they be?"

Dewayne said, "I'll tell you exactly who it is. It's that goddamned LAPD Metro bunch. They come down here in our territory, and they shoot up our citizens, and then they move out like a phantom because they don't want to have to write reports of a shot fired." So they helped us, but they didn't want to get into all that paperwork that goes on when you have to explain why you used a gun.

When we shook John Stanley down, we found both his front pants pockets loaded with heroin packets. And in the web between the thumb and forefinger of his right hand was a big scar, a bite mark like Alma Tabori described that wasn't healed yet. So we took him in and booked him for eleven rapes, assault on a police officer, attempted murder and narcotics.

And we relaxed; the summertime rape epidemic was all wrapped up.

Four days later we got a call: attempted rape on North Lapeer Drive, the suspect was now running down Lapeer. We put every unit on it, and five minutes later one of the beat units bagged the bastard.

When Zenter and I walked up to him on the scene, we couldn't believe it. The guy was an exact double for John Stanley, who was already in custody. He even had the identical bite mark on his right hand! So much coincidence is incredible, but there was the proof it could happen.

Two days Ed and I spent in the interrogation room with this guy, Dan Michaels, and finally he went for everything. He signed a confession and told us the whole story.

He was a street sweeper in Century City, the big luxury office and hotel and condominium development that's built on what used to be the old Twentieth Century-Fox back lot. This is just west of Beverly Hills. And Michaels lived in the Wilshire district of LA, which is just east of Beverly Hills.

Every day he got off work at eleven in the morning, he ate his lunch, and he walked home through Beverly Hills. And every day he knocked on a door or two in Beverly Hills, and almost every day he raped somebody.

Then he went on home to his wife and two kids. His wife was a lovely woman, and the kids were great, and I never could understand why he would take the chance of hurting them like he did. But then I never could understand anybody who commits rape.

We prosecuted Michaels, but first I had to go down to the court in Compton and get the rape charges dismissed against John Stanley, who was the wrong man. The reason he ran from us was the narcotics, not rape.

The judge in Compton, Homer L. Garrott, was a young black guy who had not been on the bench too long, and he really chewed out Stanley for that street scene on Imperial Highway that could have turned into a massacre. He read Stanley a lecture that ought to be in every judge's repertoire.

"I want to tell you something," he said to the guy, "and I want you to pay attention. The Beverly Hills Police Department had a warrant for your arrest when they came looking for you. And when the police come after you with a warrant, you surrender. *You* do not decide whether you should be placed under arrest, you don't fight back, you don't try to escape, you do whatever they order you to do. And you fight your case in the court, not in the street. Do you understand?"

Stanley mumbled something, and Judge Garrott said, "Now, it's in your favor that they are withdrawing their charges against you, but I am holding you, and you will be tried on all of the other charges."

That kind of thing happens so seldom in any court anymore that I went back to Judge Garrott's chambers afterward to commend him personally.

I said, "Judge, I wish you were sitting in Beverly Hills in-

stead of Compton, because if this was Beverly Hills, all but
one of our judges, knowing we didn't have the right rape
suspect, would have thrown the whole thing out. I like the
way you read the law."

And he said, "Well, too many people who create violence
in the streets do so because they feel that they can get justice there. But they can't, and they have to somehow learn
that they can't."

I don't know Judge Garrott's background, but I'd be willing to bet that he's like most other black people: He got
maybe too little justice when he grew up, but that way he
learned the value of it.

In another rape case that we had, the guy would kidnap a
girl in an alley at night. He would force her to get into his
car, rape her and then make her give him a head job, beat
and rob her and, finally, throw her out of his car and drive
off. He did all this several times, with different girls.

One night he hit Beverly Hills, and he went into an alley
and strong-armed Greta Gustafson, who was a secretary to
Alan Ladd's son, Alan, Junior. But the guy was bothered by
too much activity in the alley, too many open windows and
people around, and he split before he completed the whole
MO. All he did was rob her.

About a month later I picked up a teletype where a guy
followed a girl into an alley in Gardena the same way. After
almost all night of this he kicked her out of his car on Imperial Highway just before daylight.

The girl, Goldie Elton, had the presence of mind to write
down the guy's license number as he drove off. She wrote it
in lipstick on the mirror of her compact—SPY 899, a California plate.

There was no such plate; it didn't exist. Gardena stopped
investigating there; I don't know why, but maybe it's because Gardena is the big town for legal poker parlors, and
they never want to admit that they have any crime there.

So I started juggling numbers and letters in all kinds of

combinations, and finally, I ran SRY 899, and it came back an Oldsmobile that LAPD Rampart Division had impounded in a burglary case and that had been lent to a guy named Jim Grimes by a body and fender shop.

At Rampart I talked to their detective on the case. I inquired about that P that might be an R.

He said, "Oh, yeah. Until we pulled the little piece of tape off that covered the tail of the R, it looked like a P. We couldn't make the guy, so we wrote him a ticket for misuse of the plate."

He never mentioned that in the teletype, which is why I had to waste a couple of days trying to find a P that was really an R. He could have saved me the trouble.

He could have looked a little closer at the car, too, because down behind the driver's seat I found Greta Gustafson's keys. The guy used the same borrowed car in both jobs.

Now that I had got through this confusion and knew the guy I was looking for, there were the usual problems. I found Grimes' mother, down on Manchester Avenue, but she wouldn't give me the temperature in a blizzard.

So finally, I stiffed in a call to her and said, "Hey, Mama, this is Leroy. I'm in county jail, and I'm going to get out tomorrow, and I hear through the grapevine that the police is looking for Jim."

"That's right," she said. "I know the police is looking for Jim. They talked to me." Of course, I was the one that had talked to her.

I said, "Mama, the police is going to kill him. He don't know what I know, and I got to get him and talk to him."

"Well," she said, "he ain't going to come back here."

So I said, "I'm going to get out at five tomorrow, so you tell him I'll call, I got to talk to him."

"Okay," she said, "I'll tell him."

I got to be the department expert at playing Leroy and Willie like that, even when it wasn't my case. Another time some of the guys went down in the black ghetto looking for a pimp-forger with the street name of Leroy. They knocked on a door, and there was no answer. So Roger Bedford got on the radio.

"Have Franklin stiff in a call to this number and ask for Leroy," he said. "And if Leroy is there, let us know, and we'll kick the door in." They didn't want to kick the door and find nobody there.

I dialed the number, and a woman, sounding like an older woman, came on the phone. I said, "Hey, Mama, this is Willie. Let me talk to Leroy."

She said, "Okay," and I heard her yell, "Leroy! Telephone!"

He came to the phone and said, "Yeah?" They will come to the phone, but they won't go to the door.

I said, "Leroy, go open the motherfucking door before the police kick it in."

He said, "What?"

And I said, "Hey, man, go open the door. The police are going to kick it if you don't open it."

"There ain't no police at my door, man," he said.

"Do me a favor," I said. "Leave the phone off the hook and go to the door and see who's there."

I heard him walking across the room and opening the door, and I heard Roger yell something at him.

And Leroy started in, "Hey, man, what is this? What is this?"

"We've been knocking on the door here for half an hour," Roger said. "Why didn't you open the door?"

Leroy said, "Man, I didn't know you was knocking on the door. I'm just talking to my friend Willie on the telephone. I been talking to him for half an hour."

So Roger came over to the phone and picked it up and said, "Okay, thanks, Willie." And he hung up.

On the rape investigation where I had played Leroy for Jim Grimes' mother, the next night we went down to the

Jim Dandy Fried Chicken—it's at Manchester and Western avenues—and I got on the phone and did my Leroy bit once more.

"Mama," I said, "this is Leroy again, I just got out of jail. I got to talk to him."

She said, "He's not here right now."

"Okay," I said. I told her where I was and said, "I'm going to stay here one hour. He better come down here and see me in one hour."

She said, "Okay."

We waited and we watched the Jim Dandy Fried Chicken. After about twenty minutes a Cadillac pulled up alongside the place, a guy got out, and he was a walking picture of Jim Grimes. Two girls in the car.

I got out from my stakeout point, and I walked in behind him, looking out of place because I was the only white dude in there. He turned around, took one look at me and split to run. So I grabbed him right there.

"Hey, man," he said, "I'm not Jim. I'm Jim's brother. You're not looking for me."

Campbell came over, and we talked to the guy out by his car, and I said, "I don't know how much you love your brother, but the guy has committed a vicious crime, and we're going to kill the son of a bitch."

One of the girls popped up with, "Oh, I hope you don't! You guys just killed one of my brothers last year. I hope you ain't going to kill another one."

They admitted that they had been talking with him. So I told the girl, "I'm going to go back to Beverly Hills, and I'm going to wait until twelve midnight. If he doesn't call me by twelve midnight, I'm going to put out a pickup on him, and with the viciousness of the crime, he's going to be shot."

About eleven o'clock the phone rang in Beverly Hills, and the guy said, "Hey, this is Jim. Can I come over and talk to you tomorrow?"

I said, "No. You can come over and talk to me tonight."

Thirty minutes later he walked in, and by morning he had copped out to everything: the Greta Gustafson robbery in Beverly Hills, where he admitted he had planned to rape her but got scared off; the Goldie Elton rape in Gardena where we got the license number; and another rape of a black girl named Doris Beauchamp that happened in South Central LA.

We filed everything on him, we went to Superior Court in LA, and the hassles began. Only this time we had a good judge, William Drake.

The defense took the usual malarkey line that a black man is always unfairly accused and a white man will never give him an even break. We had a mostly white jury, so the defense attorney started screaming about that.

"Here we've got a Mississippi jury and a Mississippi cop handling the case," he said, "and we just can't get a fair trial here at all. I'm not even going to come back at two o'clock this afternoon to try the case."

Judge Drake reminded me of Charlton Heston playing God, the way he looked down at the guy from the bench, and when he spoke, you felt like looking up at the ceiling to see if thunder clouds were forming. "Counsel," he said, "we all have problems. But you *will* come back at two o'clock, and you *will* try the case to the best of your ability. And I don't expect to have to say any more on that subject."

The guy came back at two o'clock.

But out in the corridor at recess time the hassling went on, just like it did when the friends of Beardsley Cheney, Jr., and Hal Fulliam hassled my victims in that robbery case. This time it was the family and friends of Jim Grimes standing close by and talking loud so Greta Gustafson and Goldie Elton would be sure to hear them.

"Well, man, look at all them honkies in there," they said. "You got a Mississippi jury, you got a Mississippi cop running the case, and it don't matter if Jim is guilty or not— they're going to railroad him anyway. But you just wait.

Our day is going to come. Our *day* is going to *come!*" They
kept hammering away at that, trying to intimidate these
girls their pal had robbed and raped.

I took the DA with me, and we went in to see Judge
Drake in his chambers. I told him what was going on, and I
said, "Your Honor, we don't have to put up with this. If the
court can't take some action, I will take some action. I will
arrest them on the spot."

Judge Drake called everybody into the courtroom, and he
advised them from the bench that if he got another report of
them hassling my witnesses or me or the DA or anybody
else connected, he would hold them in contempt and have
them taken out and booked for intimidation and obstructing justice.

That shut them up. All it ever takes to shut up that kind
of people is an honest judge who applies the law evenly to
both the prosecution and the defense.

We convicted Jim Grimes on the Goldie Elton kidnap-
rape-robbery case, but that was all. We didn't convict him
on the Greta Gustafson robbery because of one black juror,
who argued like hell and raised a question whether I had
planted her keys in that borrowed car. One of the jurors, a
woman, got Greta's telephone number from the DA and
called her and told her that.

And we didn't convict Grimes of the kidnap-rape-robbery
of Doris Beauchamp because she wouldn't testify. It was
not because she was scared or ashamed or any of the usual
reasons that a woman backs off from facing a guy that raped
her.

"He's the guy, isn't he?" I said.

"Yeah," she said, "he's the guy, but I won't testify."

"Look," I said, "is there more to this than I know? Is he
an old boyfriend or something?"

She said, "No, I never saw him before that night. And
now don't you go asking if I liked it, because I didn't, I hate
the son of a bitch!"

"Then why won't you testify?"

"Why, man," she said, "he's black. I can't come down there and testify against a soul brother."

She was so goddamned brainwashed by that black philosophy that she would rather be raped than right. Nobody can fashion justice out of that kind of material.

12

Breaking the Monotony

CAR CHASES are exciting; they break the monotony of a cop's routine, which is mostly like army routine: sit around and wait. But car chases don't have much to do with police work.

Most of the cop series on TV are ridiculous because they are cheap shots at making movies. The script writer types a one-liner like "Baretta chases the crook," and that takes up ten minutes of action film, the meaning of which is that the writer doesn't know anything about police work and he doesn't have an idea for a story.

The average cop gets into maybe two to four chases in twenty years, and as a chase cop I'm just average. The wildest chase I was ever in, I was after Elvis Presley's Maserati.

Elvis had just bought the car, and somebody backed into it while it was parked and bashed up the left front fender and headlight. Elvis took it in for the repairs, and come Sunday a mechanic named Hans Bettenheim took it out to show to a friend. Hans was not just a mechanic; he was also a sports car race driver from Germany. He could handle a Maserati, one of the fastest cars in the world, better than I can breathe.

Hans and his friend were driving up Benedict Canyon when the light at Lexington Road turned red on them, but Hans rolled right on through because he was going too fast anyway. I happened to be right there on Lexington, so I went after him to make a routine pullover.

Instead, I got myself into a Grand Prix. When I laid the flasher on him, he took off up the mountain like a Baptist preacher on his way to meet St. Peter.

I hit the siren and gave it the lead foot, but I might as well have been driving a 1916 electric sedan with a flower vase at the window. It was a thirty-five-mile zone, and I was doing eighty and speeding up, and the Maserati was pulling away like I was in reverse.

Judge Adolph Alexander was sitting on the bench in Beverly Hills at the time, and he happened to be up in the canyon at his nephew's house, watering the shrubbery. I got a glimpse of him as we went by like a couple of cannonballs, and his mouth was wide open in astonishment and his eyebrows were clear on top of his head.

Benedict Canyon is a two-lane road with hairpin turns as sharp as 180 degrees, but the Maserati didn't even seem to slow down. I chased him over the top of the Santa Monica Mountains, up Benedict, along Mulholland and down Beverly Glen into the San Fernando Valley at Sherman Oaks.

When I got to Mulholland and Beverly Glen, at the top of the mountain where I could look down the other side, the Maserati was a mile ahead of me. It started out a block ahead.

So I went downhill, and I radioed for a roadblock; we could trap the guy in the canyon, but if he got out onto the floor of the San Fernando Valley, he had a million escape routes. That valley, which is a fourth of Los Angeles, is as big as the entire city of Chicago.

He got out. I went all the way to Ventura Boulevard, he could have turned off several places, and there was no roadblock. And no Maserati either.

I spotted an LAPD sergeant, and I said, "Where's the road-block?"

He said, "What do you mean, roadblock?"

Then I found out my radio wasn't working; nobody got my message. So I started back over to Beverly Hills.

When I got to the top of the mountain, my radio came in again; I guess the mountain had cut off the signal. "One of the traffic units has your Maserati at Camden and Carmelita," the dispatcher said.

That German buzz bomb was already back in Beverly Hills and busted for several minutes, and I was only half-way home. It turned out he had ducked into a little dead-end street on the Valley side; then he headed back after I went by.

"Why did you split like that?" I said to him. "You traded a red-light ticket for a bucket of trouble. Why?"

"I was so scared when you came after me," he said. "I didn't want the boss to know that I had taken out the car without permission."

I filed everything in the vehicle code against Hans Betten-heim, including grand theft auto. But his boss backed off on that charge; he wouldn't complain.

We went to court, and the judge was the astonished guy who was watering his nephew's shrubbery, Adolph Alexander. In the legal proceedings I had never mentioned that the judge was a witness to the chase.

"Your Honor," the defense attorney said, "my client is a sports car race driver, he's a mechanic, he knows these roads and he knows the Maserati, and he can drive at seventy miles an hour safer than the average person can drive twenty-five."

Judge Alexander slammed his fist down on the bench hard enough to crack bricks. "Nobody!" he said. "Nobody! Nobody can drive over Benedict Canyon as fast as this maniac was driving. I saw it, and when that Maserati went by, I thought it was a stampeding herd of cattle! And then the police car, the same thing. You're lucky nobody got killed!"

The judge made a point of looking up the maximum penalty for every charge, and he gave Hans the biggest fine for a traffic violation I ever heard of; I think it was $1,000. And he found that under certain circumstances he could revoke the guy's driver's license for two years instead of the usual one year, so he took Hans off the road for two years.

"And at the end of that revocation," Judge Alexander said, "I'm going to reinstate and then revoke for a second two years."

All of which only shows that when a judge really knows what's going on in the streets, he gets tougher than a sandwich of tenpenny nails.

Another sports car race driver, Jimmy Jurgensen, who had a sideline of smashing windows to steal furs, liked to wait until a cop came around before he'd pull a job, just for the fun of getting away in the chase. He boasted about hitting fur shops when there was a police car across the street.

Jimmy had a souped-up Corvette that was hotter than a traveling salesman's wife on Friday night, and he had it specially equipped so he could dive into it headfirst, hit the gas pedal with his hand and take off.

Every night Jimmy would smash a sidewalk window somewhere, grab two or three mink stoles off mannequins, and split. If he was rushed, he'd throw a whole mannequin in the Corvette and take the fur off later.

One night I was staked on H. W. Blaine Furs, down on Olympic, and almost every other fur shop in Beverly Hills was staked. And Jimmy hit a shop up on Wilshire that we hadn't staked.

We had figured the most likely place he'd leave town would be at La Cienega and Olympic, so I went over there to intercept him. Half an hour later nothing had showed up, so I went back to Blaine Furs and the window was smashed and cleaned out. If I had stayed at my spot, I'd have been right on him.

Another night he hit a shop on Rodeo Drive directly across from the Luau, where we had a unit staked out. He pulled up about three in the morning, he got out of the Corvette with a two-by-four in his hand and he smashed the window.

Paul McEwen jumped into the middle of the street with a shotgun and yelled, "Police officer!"

Jimmy just threw that mannequin into the Corvette, dived in headfirst and took off. Paul emptied the shotgun into the back of the car, but all he did was knock out a tail-light and mess up the mannequin's hairdo. If Jimmy had been sitting in the driver's seat instead of lying down, he'd have had his head blown all over Rodeo Drive.

Jimmy hit the upgrade to the railroad tracks northbound on Rodeo, flew clear across Santa Monica Boulevard airborne and was gone.

A taxi driver who was at the corner there said, "Man, oh, man! When that Corvette went by here, that crazy girl driving it was really leaning back! How come you cops let people like that drive around and kill the rest of us?"

All I could think of to say was, "Hey, fellow, she's a real doll."

Nobody ever caught Jimmy in a chase, but finally, he made a mistake. He had a steady girlfriend, a stripper who called herself Lacey Pantees, and he made the mistake of giving a mink stole to another girl he was playing around with.

Lacey came into the station one morning in a tight sweater that was all ajuggle, and she said, "You want a guy for smashing windows in fur stores?"

We didn't say no.

"Okay," she said. "That son of a bitch, he just crossed me. His garage looks like a fur store. Come out and look for yourself."

She was right: Jimmy's double garage was loaded with racks of furs like a discount house. He was hitting every night and selling them as fast as he could; but he couldn't sell them fast enough, and he had developed a warehouse problem.

So we busted Jimmy Jurgensen, but not in a chase. We did it the only way we could, standing still.

For some reason Lacey Pantees made it part of the deal that she got a job as a clerk in the Beverly Hills Police Department, so we hired her. But she wasn't too efficient with her clothes on, and we had to fire her.

The craziest chase I ever got into happened when a guy named Todd Birdsall walked into a jewelry store on North Beverly Drive one early evening in Christmas season and robbed it of four diamond rings worth about $20,000.

Birdsall ran out and jumped into his car, where his girlfriend, Evelyn Welker, was waiting. He handed her the rings, and they took off down Beverly Drive.

The 211 was out in about a minute, and a beat guy spotted Birdsall's car and went in pursuit. Ed Zenter and I happened to be about a block away, and we took off in pursuit of the pursuit.

But we had a problem. We were working a vice detail that evening, and we were the most unlikely-looking cops you ever saw. We were all duded up in flashy clothes, and we were driving a wild purple convertible with a white top which was down. In the department we call it the Purple Phantom. We looked like maybe we belonged in a movie about Hollywood, but not in a police chase. Not even in a Hollywood movie about a police chase.

So we were barreling down Beverly Drive and coming up on the Wilshire intersection. Birdsall sailed through on the green light; the beat unit barely made it; we hit the red. We tried to keep going, but we had no siren, no red flasher, no ID that anybody could see. Suddenly we were just two dudes in a purple convertible that had just created a huge traffic jam in the middle of the crossroads at Beverly and

Wilshire. We couldn't move an inch; we were the stars in a Mack Sennett comedy.

Zenter was furious. He stood up in the car, shook his fist at the other drivers around us and yelled, "Goddammit, you stupid idiots! Can't you see that this is a police car?"

Finally, we squeezed through, and with the beat units we trapped Birdsall and his girlfriend in a dead-end street and forced him to wreck his car. Birdsall got away in the darkness, we couldn't find the diamonds, but we got the girl.

And from her we located their Hollywood pad. We kicked in the door, and right away the phone rang. Zenter and I both grabbed for it, but I was closer and I got it, and a guy said, "Hey, man, that whole thing went wrong. We pulled the job, we got four diamond rings, but the police got after us, and we busted the buggy. The cops are all over the place; you got to come get me."

He seemed to think that I was a friend of his, so I said, "Okay, where are you?"

He said, "I'll be in the Parisian Room." That's a coffee shop at La Brea and Washington.

So I said, "Okay, man, twenty minutes." I hung up, and I said to Zenter, "The guy wants transportation."

"All right," Ed said, "but, you son of a bitch, I'll get even." He was talking about me grabbing the phone first, and it took awhile, but he did get even on the ski-mask case.

We went down to the Parisian Room, and Birdsall was sitting at the counter. I walked over and put a gun on him, and we took him in.

But the four diamonds were still missing. It was a couple of days before Evelyn Welker would tell us where they were.

"You know the patrol car that took me in after you arrested me?" she said.

I said, "No, but I can find it."

"Look behind the backseat," she said. "I slipped the rings into my panties just before you busted me. You handcuffed me behind my back, and when the other guys were taking me in, I got the rings out of my panties, and I slid them down behind the seat."

That's where we found them. That patrol car had been sitting around and running around for two days in all kinds of situations and with all kinds of people in it and with $20,000 worth of diamond rings under the backseat for anybody to reach down and find and walk off with. We were just lucky.

Lester Irwin wasn't so lucky. Lester owned the store that Birdsall ripped off, and Lester filed a loss statement of $70,000. Lester never dreamed that we would catch the people and recover the property, so he didn't appreciate the good news when I brought it to him.

"Mr. Irwin," I said, "we have caught the people that robbed you, and we have made a full recovery of the four rings, which have been appraised at twenty thousand dollars."

His Palm Springs tan suddenly turned to a kind of Folsom flush.

"Evidently you made a little mistake in your crime report," I said. "You reported a loss of seventy thousand dollars, and the full recovery of the four rings that were taken amounts to only twenty thousand dollars by official appraisal. In the heat of excitement we all make mistakes, Mr. Irwin. Maybe you should recheck your inventory."

I was giving him an out, and he grabbed it.

"Mr. Franklin," he said, "I'm delighted to hear that you've recovered my property. And if you say I've made a mistake in inventory, I'll correct it. I'm sure that whatever you say is right."

This was the same bastard who once bought a $3,000 watch that had been stolen from Harmon Bellows, a very big corporate lawyer in Beverly Hills. A guy walked in off the street, and Irwin bought the watch for $150, no questions asked. I came in, identified it, seized it and took it back to Harmon, no questions asked.

Irwin is always making little mistakes like that. But this time he stopped trying to rip off his insurance company.

We convicted Birdsall and Welker; he went to prison, and she went to a halfway house for hypes. But like I said, car chases don't have much to do with police work. Especially if the car is a purple convertible.

13

The Tiffany Caper

BENTON JONES got into bad company down in New Orleans, so his folks sent him to LA to get him away from his friends that were thieves and hypes, and in LA he got in with worse.

The first thing he did, he was walking with his girlfriend in an alley near her house in Leimert Park, and he saw a brand-new bright-red Oldsmobile Toronado just asking to be stolen. So he stole it. He got into the car with a coat hanger, he found an ignition key in the glove compartment, and he took his girl for a joy ride. They drove out to Santa Monica and had a few drinks, and when they got back to her house, she said, "Benton, I got to introduce you to somebody."

She took him down the street and introduced him to Joe Black and his brother Truman Black, Jr., and she said, "Guess what? Benton's got some wheels!"

Joe Black looked out the window and saw the wheels. "Man!" he said to Benton Jones. "You're in! We need somebody with wheels, and you are now a member of us."

"What are you talking about?" Benton said.

Joe said, "We're going to pull a job. We're going to hit Tiffany's on Wilshire Boulevard."

187

"You're crazy, man!" Benton said. "That's in Beverly Hills, and we heard about the Beverly Hills Police Department in New Orleans. You can't get away with that."

"Man," said Joe, "we're going to make a big splash. We're going to hit Beverly Hills, and we're going to get away with it."

First thing they needed was handguns. Joe and some of his friends had been pulling shotgun robberies in South Central LA, so Joe and Jimson Biggs walked into Bill's Sporting Goods Store on South Broadway, laid shotguns on the people there and walked out with thirteen handguns.

Wednesday, which was the day before Thanksgiving, seven of them drove up to Tiffany's, on Wilshire at El Camino in a corner of the Beverly Wilshire Hotel building. They parked in the red zone on the side street, and Franklin Ledbetter and another guy I could never get an ID on stayed outside on lookout. Joe Black and Truman and their younger brother, Wilson Black, and Benton Jones and Jimson Biggs went into the store.

There were maybe thirty people in the place, clerks and customers like Dom de Luise the actor and three or four security guards. The guards carried no guns; they were just a psychological force standing around to keep the wealthy kleptomaniac customers from shoplifting—some of them would buy a $1,000 watch and try to steal a $19.95 compact.

But the guards did carry ADT monitors, and if they pressed the button, the alarm sounded in a security office that notified police.

Five black guys wearing uptown Saturday Night duds and walking into a store like Tiffany's all at once—they looked like they got off the train at the wrong station.

One of the guards, a black guy with the great name of Le Scorpio St. Thomastein, told me afterward, "Man, as soon as they walked in, I knew something was wrong. I was standing there with my monitor in my hand and my finger on the button, waiting for something to happen."

It didn't happen for a couple of minutes, while they acted like customers. Truman Black, Jr., walked up to another guard, a sixty-five-year-old guy named Charles Burk, pointed to a case full of watches and said, "How much are those watches there?"

Burk said, "I don't know. You'll have to ask one of the clerks."

Truman went back to look at the watches again. Then he pointed to one of them, and he asked Burk again, "How much is that right there?"

"I'm sorry," Burk said, "I tell you I don't know. You'll have to talk to one of the clerks."

With that Truman reached into his coat for his gun, and before he got it out, he yelled, "Goddamn, man, this is a robbery!"

And across the room Benton Jones pulled a gun and yelled, "Hit the floor, everybody! This is a robbery!"

Joe Black fired some shots at the walls and the ceiling, and everybody hit the floor but Old Man Burk. He tried to grab Truman's gun, and they wrestled for it for two or three seconds, and then Truman shot him in the chest, right under the heart. And as the old man went down, he put his hand up to ward off another blow, and Truman shot him again, in the hand.

I asked Burk later why he did it, and he said, "I almost got it away. I thought how embarrassing it's going to be for me, being here as security and letting those guys rob the place." He is tough as a cob; they got him out to UCLA Emergency, and he pulled through okay, except that he still has some pains in his chest.

St. Thomastein hit the floor with everybody else, but he was pressing that button. "I just held it all the time while I was on the floor," he said. And a guy named Robert Valley, across Wilshire at the Rolls-Royce place, phoned the department that there was shooting at Tiffany's; that was how we got the first report.

"Smash the display cases!" one of the robbers screamed,

and they started smashing the cases and stuffing diamonds and watches into a couple of pillowcases they had brought in under their coats.

Suddenly one of them yelled, "Let's get out of here; we're being surrounded!"

And they split, swinging those pillowcases full of loot, and they piled into the red Toronado and headed south on El Camino.

We missed them by maybe thirty seconds. Robert Valley told me that as they got in the car on the side street, one of our patrol units was pulling to the curb on Wilshire in front of the building. That was Bob O'Connor, who is strictly a traffic officer, and it was probably a good thing he was a little late because he is better with a ticket book or a golf club than with a gun, and they probably would have killed him.

When the radio dispatcher came on with, "Shots fired, two eleven in progress, Tiffany's!" I was just three blocks away on Charleville, checking out a purse snatch.

I might even have passed the bastards on the way because they hadn't been gone a minute when I got to Tiffany's and found everything smashed up and Old Man Burk lying all bloody on the floor.

That was the beginning of an investigation that took ten months and used up a lot of my patience with the law. At the time I didn't figure it would take that long; they got away with $451,000 in diamond jewelry and watches, but the job was sloppy as hell. That told me right off I was dealing with gutter minds, and gutter minds are never very smart. But there are a lot of frustrations in detective work, and I ran into most of them on this case. I also got twenty death threats.

Right at first we were into the tedious routine of interviewing witnesses, getting descriptions, finding evidence, calling people and getting out teletypes to other police agencies.

Many witnesses that are eager to help at first will back off

after they have time to think it over. We found the Toronado abandoned in an alley off South Camden Drive about ten
minutes after the robbery, and a woman there told us she
saw two black guys run out of the alley and get into a red
Mustang driven by a third guy. But later the woman refused
to testify on the advice of her son, who is a public defender.
A real good citizen, that guy.

And Dom de Luise wouldn't help us when I wanted to
come over and show him some mug shots.

"I'm sorry," he said, "but I couldn't identify anyone.
When they came in there and said, 'Hit the floor!' I jumped
to the ceiling and bounced off before I hit the floor." He had
to be funny, even on the phone to a cop. "I wouldn't know if
they were black or white," he said.

I reminded him, "You told me you could identify them."

"I know, but I really couldn't," he said. "But good luck to
you, I hope you get every one of those motherfuckers."

Now why would he use black language like that if he
didn't know they were black?

That first night four of us worked all night. About ten
o'clock Chief Cork called to find out how things were going.

"We're at a dead end," I said. "But we're still on it."

"Let me talk to Lieutenant Princeton," he said.

I said, "He's not here."

"Where is he?"

"What do you mean, where is he?" I said. "You know
where Princeton is; he's at home."

Cork said, "You've got to be kidding."

And I said, "You know damned well he went home at
four o'clock this afternoon. I had a hell of a time justifying
staying on myself."

We had been having a big hassle about overtime, and
Lieutenant Princeton was always the best clock watcher in
the department. It bugged the hell out of me because you
can't solve crimes on an eight-hour day or any other kind of

timetable. You get a purse snatch and a license number at four o'clock in the afternoon, and Princeton will say, "Okay, we'll run a DMV on it, and first thing tomorrow morning we'll go down and try to pick the people up." By morning they'll be rid of the evidence, but if you get on it right away and damn the overtime, sometimes they've still got the purse and everything in the car, and you grab them and that prevents twelve more purse snatches.

But the city fathers think that because you can run a rug business or a dress boutique on regular hours, you can do the same with detective work, so they're always objecting to overtime, and Princeton goes along with that.

So now Chief Cork said, "How many guys you got working with you?"

I said, "Three." I had Campbell and Zenter and Griffey.

And he said, "Look, call in anybody you want. And Princeton will be back within the hour."

"Hey, Chief," I said, "tomorrow is Thanksgiving Day."

"So what?" he said.

I said, "It'll be double time and a half day, Thanksgiving."

"To hell with you, guy!" he said. "You're not going to even see Thanksgiving. I don't want to catch you eating any turkey until this thing is over, see?"

About midnight we all went down to LASO Firestone Division to start contacting snitches. Most of those guys you can't reach by phone; you've got to go find them. And after we got all the routine stuff out of the way, it was either sit around and wait or develop something on your own.

When we walked in, Dewayne Primesburger took one look at Zenter and me and said, "Oh, God, no! Every time you guys come down here, all hell breaks loose!" Dewayne can never forget that night we chased John Stanley down Imperial Highway through a thousand people, and every time we go down to LASO Firestone we go through this routine.

"Hey, Dewayne," I said, "this is a good case. We're just looking for some people."

"Yeah, sure," he said. "I better issue body armor to the entire citizenry."

We got busy, and we were beginning to get callbacks from snitches, and then I got a call from Lieutenant Princeton. "I'm at the station," he said, like nothing had ever happened. "When will you be back?"

"I don't know," I said. "We're working on something. We may be back sometime tomorrow."

"Well," he said, "I'll tell you what, why don't you come on back now? We'll reevaluate where we are, and then we can go from there." Cork got him out of bed, and he wanted to go back.

I said, "Look, we got some things to do. If you want to, come down and join us, but we got some things going."

A couple of hours later he came down to Firestone, and we worked through Thanksgiving morning, and finally we got a little sleep, which I needed more than turkey, and then back to work.

That afternoon Larry Carroll from Channel 7 came out to Beverly Hills to interview me for the news, and he asked me if I thought the job was well planned and organized.

I said, "No, Larry, it's not organized, there's no planning at all; it's just a bunch of stupid, disorganized thieves."

Later on Benton Jones told me that he and a bunch of the thieves were watching TV that night, and that comment of mine made Joe Black madder than all hell. Joe had set himself up to the others as a big-time robber, well organized, and he didn't like hearing different.

It was two thirty in the morning after Thanksgiving that we got our first real tip. I was working down in Compton, and Sergeant Fred Koch took a call from one of my snitches, a girl.

"If you want to know where the people that ripped off

194 | SAWED-OFF JUSTICE

Tiffany's are," she said, "you ought to be at a house on Deg-
nan Boulevard at six o'clock in the morning. They'll be
there. They'll probably be driving a red Mustang. One of
them's name is Joe, and the other one, Benton, has got a big
space between his teeth."

Some of the witnesses at Tiffany's had told us one of the
guys had a big space between his front teeth. And the Deg-
nan Boulevard address she gave us was in Leimert Park,
only two blocks from where the Toronado getaway car was
stolen, at Eleventh and Vernon. And here again was mention of a red Mustang.

It looked good, so Koch got a couple of our uniformed
guys down there, Bob Froschauer and John Gould, and they
staked on the house with LAPD backup.

At six thirty in the morning a red Mustang pulled up behind the house, a gal driving and a guy with her. They went
in, and in a couple of minutes they came back out with
another guy, and LAPD stopped them.

The guys were Joe Black and Benton Jones, and the girl
was Jones' girlfriend that he lived with in the house there.
The red Mustang belonged to her. And Black and Jones
fitted the descriptions we got of two of the bandits. By now
Zenter and Griffey and Koch had arrived at the scene, so
they busted all three of them.

By eight o'clock Zenter and I were going to work on Joe
Black in the interrogation room in Beverly Hills. The guy
was real cocky, dressed like a dude, and he denied everything.

"Hey, man," he said, "I had nothing to do with no jewelry
robbery. Man, if that dude Benton Jones had anything to do
with it, I shouldn't have been with him. If I knew he had
anything to do with that Tiffany robbery, you'd never have
caught me with him."

I'd been conned before, but he laid it on me so hard about
Jones that he just about convinced me that he had nothing
to do with it.

"Okay," I said to the jailer, "put him back and bring Jones."

Jones was a pushover. We started off telling him, "Joe thinks he shouldn't be playing around with a heavy dude like you, you having something to do with the Tiffany robbery."

That didn't work, so finally, I said, "You know, somebody's going to burn when that guard dies." That seemed to bother him.

We pushed that idea for half an hour, and suddenly he copped out. "Okay," he said, "Joe and I were in on it; we pulled the robbery. Joe was the leader." That Joe really had conned me.

But Benton wouldn't say who else was with them. "We've got an understanding," he said, and he got very dramatic, like black guys can. "When one falls, he falls alone. So I can't tell you nobody else involved."

"Okay," I said, "tell me exactly how you escaped after you did the job."

"Well, we had a stolen car," he said. He wasn't ready to admit that he had stolen it. "And we dumped it and we had a T-Bird waiting for us. I laid on the floorboard, and we drove around for a long time, and finally we stopped and we checked into a Holiday Inn. And we dumped out and checked our jewelry." He told a lot more, but he claimed not to know which Holiday Inn.

Right away I put Detective Jim Dugan to checking Holiday Inns, which around LA are thicker than tourists at the Farmers Market. And the second one Jim dialed was it, the round tower in Brentwood right beside the San Diego Freeway at Sunset Boulevard.

"Yeah," the manager, Robert Moss, said, "we had a bunch like that in here a little after two in the afternoon the day before Thanksgiving."

He remembered that the guy who checked in, who was Joe Black but used another name, had his hair done up in

SAWED-OFF JUSTICE

pigtails, and Moss thought that was odd. And he carried a
green briefcase, which, it turned out, held the jewels.

Moss looked at his blotter, and then he said, "There's
another funny thing. He wrote down a license number that
didn't make sense, so I had a bellman go down in the parking lot and check it, and it was the wrong number. I wrote
in the right number on the registration card myself."

We ran the number, and it came back to Truman Black,
Sr., the old man of the Black family, down on Hillford Avenue in Compton. The getaway T-Bird was his bird.

So now I had the jailer bring Joe Black in to talk some
more, and I said, "Benton Jones has told me the whole story. Now you sit down and tell me the story."

"What did he tell you?" he said.

I said, "All right, I am not going to con you. I am going to
tell you exactly how you did it." And I went through the
whole thing, about the T-Bird, which is his father's car, and
the Holiday Inn, all of it.

And this swanky dude finally said, "Okay, I did it." He
wouldn't name anybody else; he pulled the same line that
Benton did: "When one falls, he falls alone." But this great,
well-organized planner of a big splash robbery had already
copped out just two days after he pulled the job. Now I had
conned him.

From this I could begin to run associates. Joe Black had a
rap sheet which included such pranks as robbery, grand
theft auto and assault with intent to commit murder. He
and some other guys had been pulling shotgun jobs, so I got
their mug shots to show around, and pretty soon we had
IDs on six guys that did the Tiffany job, including Joe and
Benton Jones.

One of the six was Franklin Ledbetter, and we busted him
out of bed in his house on Eighty-fifth Street in South Central LA just one week after the robbery. He copped out, and
now we had three out of seven in the bag.

Franklin told us the other guys were holed up in a house

on Bliss Street in Compton and they had the jewels in a
green briefcase. He didn't know exactly where the house
was, but Benton Jones drew us a picture of it, and we found
it, looking exactly like the picture. Later at the trial he denied he had done that, so we produced the picture, with his
signature on it, and proved he was lying. The house was
where Truman Black, Jr., lived with his wife Loreen and
their kids.

We went to Judge Zeller for a warrant, which took six
hours. Kojak or anybody on TV can order up a warrant in
ten minutes, but what it really takes is at least four and nor-
mally six or eight hours or even more, which is why a lot of
criminals get away if you wait for a warrant. You have your
choice: Go in illegally or lose them.

We wanted to get in before nightfall because in that area
after dark you don't know what kind of snipers you're going
to run into. But with the delay on the warrant we couldn't
move in until eight o'clock at night, and we needed the
warrant so the courts wouldn't throw out anything we
found in the house.

We went to Dewayne Primesburger for backup, and after
he went through the "Oh, my God!" routine, he got serious,
and he gave us LASO's SWAT team, which was Lieutenant
Bill Reed and an eight-man flak-jacketed squad with auto-
matic weapons. So we surrounded the house on Bliss Street
like we were getting ready to hit the Normandy beaches.

Dave Griffey and I had planned to kick the door in, but
Dewayne said, "Why jeopardize your lives? I'll use the PA
system and order them out. If they don't come out, we'll
throw in tear gas, and *then* you can go kick the door."

That's the way we went. Dewayne gave the order, and all
the cars lighted up their flashers. People started running out
of their houses, but Dewayne used the bullhorn to tell them
to get off the street, and they went back into the woodwork
fast. Then Dewayne ordered anybody inside the Black
house to come out.

All of a sudden two naked people, a man and a woman, came running out with their hands up and sprawled in the street. They had been taking a bath together. I checked them, and they were nobody we wanted, and they told us nobody else was inside.

They were right; our birds had flown. They had left the day after the robbery, we found out. And we found an outline in the dust of the attic where the briefcase with the jewels had been hidden.

Two of the guys we had IDs on were Truman Black, Jr., and a younger Black brother, Wilson, so we asked for warrants on them. This time it took three days over a weekend to get the warrants. But that same weekend we had a worse frustration.

A snitch that knew me, but I couldn't make him by telephone, called me and said, "Hey, Lynn, man, you want to get those Tiffany dudes?"

"Man, I sure do," I said.

"Okay," he said. "They're dangerous SOBs, and you ought to go up to Palmdale and take a look around the Vagabond Motel. They're there, and they got the stuff with them in a little green suitcase."

This fitted in with something Benton Jones had mentioned about the Black boys' mother living up in Palmdale; she was separated from Old Man Black and living with some other guy up that way. And my snitch knew about the green briefcase, so the information sounded authentic.

It was now four o'clock on Friday afternoon, and Dave Griffey and Ed Zenter and I got ready to go to Palmdale. We were washing up and changing jackets when Lieutenant Princeton saw us and said, "Where you guys going?"

"Palmdale," I said. "We got something up there."

"No," he said, "Knock it off over the weekend. We'll get a fresh start Monday morning."

"Hey, Princeton," I said, "we got something going, some damned good stuff, and we're going up to Palmdale and work it."

And he said, "No way. We got orders. We're running up too much overtime; the case is costing too much; we're going to have to knock it off."

I said, "Who the hell is concerned about this?"

"George Morgan, the city manager, is concerned about it," Princeton said. "And the City Council is upset; they're jumping all over the chief; he's jumping all over me. So knock it off."

Zenter said, "We'll do it on our own. We won't even charge the city for it."

Princeton said, "No, no way. I got orders; now you've got orders. Go home. Quit until Monday morning."

So we called it quits. None of us had had enough sleep in the days since the robbery, but waiting through that weekend was as frustrating as an itch in the middle of your back.

Monday morning early we drove up to the Vagabond Motel in Palmdale, and we showed pictures of our suspects to the man and his wife that ran the place.

He said, "Yeah, that whole bunch spent the weekend here. The last of them left about an hour ago, as soon as the gas stations opened. They had an even number, and they couldn't buy any gas yesterday." This was during the Arab oil embargo, when we had odd and even number days for buying gas according to license plate.

If we had come up Friday, we'd have grabbed Truman Black, Jr., and Loreen and Wilson Black and Jimson Biggs, who had his girlfriend with him. And we'd have grabbed the green suitcase and made a full recovery of the jewels. But overtime was more important, so it took nine more goddamned months to clean up the case, which cost the city treasury a small fortune compared to what the overtime would have been.

But that same Monday we did get Jimson Biggs. He and his girlfriend had left the motel in Palmdale on Sunday—he had an odd number—and Sunday night he did a little too much celebrating. About two o'clock Monday morning he managed to weave so far off the road in Compton that he

ran into a car that was parked in a driveway. He tried to get
away, but Compton police caught him at the scene.

Then he tried to throw away a couple of things, but the
officers picked them up—a key to Room 205 in the Vagabond Motel in Palmdale and a book of matches from the
motel.

I had a pickup out on Biggs, so Compton held him for me.
But I couldn't get much out of the guy that we didn't already know. "I was there in the robbery," he said, "but I did
not shoot the dude." Nobody knew anything about who
shot Charlie Burk.

Now the case was two weeks old, and we had four people
in custody and two more wanted, Truman Black, Jr., and
Wilson Black.

I was trying to get something on Old Man Black, too. I
had a white snitch who liked one of the Black girls, and he
was in the old man's house in Compton on Thanksgiving
Day.

"And, man," he said, "when Joe walked in, I couldn't believe it. He has got this green briefcase, and he dumps it out
on the living-room floor, and it's more jewelry than I ever
saw in my life. It's the Tiffany stuff."

He said Old Man Black looked at the stuff and got up,
held his head and said, "Oh, my God, here I'm trying to
make an honest living at narcotics and stuff, and you stupid
dudes have to go out and rob a jewelry store. Well, I guess
I'll just have to take over."

So the Old Man wasn't in it, but he was in charge now. I
kept going down and talking to him, but I never got much
of anything out of him. I kicked in his door a couple of
times, and he had a girlfriend, and I kicked in her door three
times, and I always found him there.

The girlfriend was on welfare, but she had three color TV
sets and beautiful furniture. One time I even found $300 in
$20 bills under a rug and 500 sets of king-sized sheets in a
closet, still wrapped in their plastic bags. She claimed she

didn't know they were there, and the Compton DA wouldn't file on it. Hell, doesn't everybody have 500 brand-new king-sized sheets stashed away in case of visitors?

We got ready to go to trial with the four in custody, and Ben Rollin, the chief defense attorney, slapped us with a 1538 motion, which turned into a police brutality charge. We get that almost every time we make an arrest the last few years. Rollin defended Old Man Black on a big narcotics case about ten years before and lost the case, and once he tried to show police brutality against Chief Cork, and he lost that one, too.

Joe Black testified that I jerked him out of his chair a couple of times and knocked him flat on his ass on the floor and that I threatened to throw him out the window and report it suicide.

Then Rollin got on the stand himself and testified that he visited Joe and Benton Jones in the Beverly Hills jail, and he said they were in such pain from Zenter and me beating them that they had to stand bent over, their faces were swollen, and their throats were so swollen they could hardly talk.

What Rollin didn't know was that a couple of hours after he had visited the jail and saw all this evidence of police brutality, we had shipped Joe and Benton down to county jail. And when you go to county jail, there is a routine: You get off the bus, and they ask if you have any complaints, any injuries, anything like that.

Joe and Benton had stepped out and said yes, so they gave them a complete physical with X rays and everything. The doctor testified that the only thing wrong with either of them was Benton had a little scratch on his cheek, which we proved he got in a street fight four days before we arrested him.

And one of the two male nurses, a black guy, got on the stand and testified that he had asked Benton Jones, "Hey, man, why did you guys come in here and claim that you had been beaten up by the police when there is nothing really wrong?"

And he testified that Benton had said, "Man, that's what our lawyer told us to say." Ben Rollin had put them up to it.

Now Judge David Semple had a few questions for Rollin, who was a close personal friend of his.

"Which side of Mr. Black's face was the most abused?" he said.

Rollin said, "Your Honor, I don't really recall."

The judge said, "You're a specialist in lawsuits of liability, are you not?"

"Yes, I am," Rollin said.

"And you made no notes?"

"No, Your Honor."

Finally the judge said, "I hate to say this, for Mr. Rollin and I have been friends for more than twenty years, but I cannot picture him witnessing these injuries, knowing that it would probably end up in a court suit later on and he would probably be handling the case and not making notes on the type of injury. And in view of the testimony from the doctor and the nurses, if I were to rule in favor of the defense, I would have to believe that the Beverly Hills Police Department and the county jail engaged in a gigantic conspiracy."

From the bench he called his good friend a liar, and he ruled against him.

After the trail was over, I ran into Judge Semple in the court cafeteria, and we talked about it, and I thanked him for that ruling.

And he said, "Well, Lynn, it just shows you what lengths some of these people will go to to discredit your testimony."

But he didn't cite anybody for contempt or ask any filing for perjury or obstructing justice. I brought that up to Bob Sills, the DA on the case, and he said, "Lynn, you've got to be kidding."

"No, I'm not kidding, Bob," I said. "Why didn't he do something?"

And Bob said, "That would be unheard of."

Maybe it ought to be heard of.

It was about this time that both Zenter and I began getting death threats. One guy called and asked the switchboard girl, "Do you have a Franklin and a Zenter in your department?"

The girl said, "Yes, but they are not on duty at this time."

And the caller said, "Well, the message is this: 'Bang-bang you're dead, motherfucker.' " And he hung up.

Somebody called Tiffany's anonymously and said, "You tell them two cops who are after my brothers that I'm going to blow their motherfucking heads off."

The girl who had answered the phone said, "Tell them yourself," and then the guy threatened to blow her head off, too.

All the calls were about the same; they're not worth repeating. And they stopped after the Tiffany case was over, which is interesting.

During the next five months we tried and convicted Joe Black, Benton Jones, Jimson Biggs and Franklin Ledbetter, but all this time we were still looking for Truman Black, Jr., and Wilson Black. And I was spending a lot of time following Loreen because we knew she was in contact with Truman.

One rainy day I had four ground units tailing her, plus Ed Zenter in a helicopter. She left the house on Bliss Street and drove to an apartment on Central Avenue. The chopper was just airborne again after refueling, so I went on by and parked. Pretty soon Ed flew over me.

"Okay," I said, "it's a gray, flat-roofed duplex about a quarter of a mile ahead of you."

They went on up and hovered right over the building, and Ed kept calling to me and saying, "I can't see any gray building."

"Ed," I said, "it's a gray building, and it's right under you. Can't you see it?"

He still couldn't see it, and this was ridiculous.

So I said, "Ed, do you see two big palm trees?"

"Yeah," he said, "they're right under me."

"That's the building," I said. She had parked under the palm trees in front, which Ed could see, but looking straight down at the building, all of it he saw was the white roof. He couldn't tell what color the walls were.

Pretty soon Loreen pulled out and went back to Bliss Street. "There's two of them getting out and going into the house," Ed said. "Looks like Loreen and a guy."

We thought it was probably Truman, so we surrounded the house and I kicked in the door. Loreen started screaming, and I heard a commotion in a bedroom, so I went in there and kicked open a closet, and here was a kid in the closet. They've got those kids trained; any time the police come around, hide. But there was nobody in the house except Loreen and the kids.

"Goddamn you!" Loreen said. "You been tailing me by helicopter and driving and everything else for ages. You know I've not been in contact with Truman."

We knew different, but we had to prove it. She finally moved from Bliss Street entirely, and I couldn't trace her for weeks until I got a call from one of my snitches, a gal who had taken a dislike to Loreen. She said it was a house down on Mace Place, in Primesburger's territory.

We'd been down so many times by now that Dewayne had quit the "Oh, my God!" routine; it was getting tired. Roger Bedford and I staked on the house with backup. We were parked behind a liquor store, and right across the street was a hot dog and hamburger joint where a bunch of real jive cats hung out. They saw us, and they knew we were the heat; they were even making jokes about it.

After a while a couple of the real swinging dudes got their Pepsi-Colas and their supersized hamburgers and came jiving across the street. One of them said, "Man, are you guys narcs?" We were sitting there, each of us with a shotgun across his lap.

Roger said, "No, we're not narcs. In fact, we're from the health department. We got information they're serving horse meat over there at the hamburger joint."

This one dude had a big mouthful of hamburger halfway down his throat, and he threw up every damned bit of it into the street, and they both took off with no more jive.

In a few minutes Loreen came out on the porch of the house and then went back in, so we went over and kicked in, and I asked where Truman was.

"Franklin," Loreen said, "you know we're not living together. You been watching my ass all these months; you know he's nowhere around."

But a crippled little old lady next door took one look at Truman's mug shot and said, "Sure, this man lives next door there. He's been living there about two months, with that woman and those kids."

I said, "Do you know where he is now?"

"He left just a short while ago," she said. "I imagine he'll be back anytime."

I went back to Loreen's and told her, "Loreen, I'm going to book you. When he comes in here, showing that you've been living together, and you knowing that I've been trying to take him into custody, I'm going to book you for harboring a fugitive."

We had the beat units back off so as not to spook Truman, and Zenter and I stayed inside the house with Loreen. I locked the door from the inside, so Truman would have to use his key to get in. This was to make it stick in court that this was where he lived. It can stand out like a stripteaser in church, but if the door isn't locked, the defense will say something like, "Well, he could have thought it was a subway station," and the judge will buy it even though we don't have a subway in LA.

About four hours we waited, and around eleven o'clock
Loreen got out her Bible, and she started praying and sing-
ing, and gradually she worked herself up into a state.

"Oh, God!" she moaned. "You know that Truman did
wrong to take all that jewelry out in Beverly Hills. Forgive
him, God, look down on him with mercy, guide him, direct
him." When we got to trial, Judge Temple Ewald surprised
me by letting me testify about that, which was Loreen's
cop-out.

A few minutes after midnight that old getaway T-Bird of
the old man's pulled into the driveway, and Truman, Jr., got
out. He put his key in the door and started to open it, and I
jerked it wide and laid the shotgun on him.

Ed was cuffing him, and we thought we were through for
the night when Dave Griffey came on the radio and said,
"There's another car pulling up in front."

Two guys got out, and one was Wilson Black, the other
guy we wanted. With him was Roland Dawkins, a big,
lanky dude who was friends with the Blacks and was also
trying to get into LAPD and become a cop. They walked almost to the steps, and then they both hesitated, like they
knew something was wrong, so I stepped out on the porch,
pumped one in and yelled, "Freeze!"

Roland, who was three or four feet behind Wilson Black,
stood on his tiptoes to see. He was about six-six to begin
with, and this made him about seven feet tall. And Roland
had the biggest, whitest teeth you ever saw, and it was
bright moonshine, and I couldn't tell if he was grinning or if
it was fright. All I could see was teeth.

For just a second Wilson acted like he was going to run,
and I was hoping he wouldn't because if he ran, and I shot, I
was going to shoot right through him and hit Roland Dawkins. I didn't want to do that because Roland is not a bad
guy. But Wilson thought better of it and raised his hands,
and that saved me a bad scene.

It was now May 31, more than six months after the robbery, and we had six guys in the bag, which is all we were ever going to get because nobody could ID the seventh. I knew who he was, but I also knew I could never get even a filing, let alone a conviction. I wouldn't waste time on him.

But there was still $451,000 in jewelry out there, and we had not recovered one diamond. This was embarrassing because twice we came so close to getting the stuff, first in Palmdale and then on Bliss Street. It was still around town somewhere; no fence would touch it because it was too hot.

What was needed now was more snitch information, which had already proved its value; of the six guys we busted, we got four directly on snitch information, and two indirectly. But all those snitches had personal reasons, like grudges.

The problem now, with everybody in jail, was that it became impersonal. Grudges didn't count.

Money did count. My snitches wanted money to tell me where the loot was. But Tiffany wouldn't pay a dime; they didn't give a damn because their insurance company had already paid them off.

And the company, which was St. Paul Insurance in New York, wouldn't go for anything either. Finally, I talked to one guy there who said, "What kind of commitment do you want?"

I said, "I want a commitment that you will pay X amount of dollars for anything recovered. I've got people trying to deal with me, and I can't even talk to them because I can't promise them anything."

"Okay," he said, "how much do you want?"

"Don't ask me what I want," I said. "It's not what I want; it's what *they* want."

"Well, then, what kind of commission do they want?"

"How about ten percent?"

He said, "How about five percent?"

"Oh, get off my goddamned back!" I said. "I wouldn't be petty enough to go out and talk to somebody about five percent. It's ten percent, or I'm going to close this case out and stop looking for jewelry if you don't care about cutting your loss."

"I'll get back to you," he said.

The next morning at eleven he called me and said, "Okay, I've got the go-ahead. Tell your people that we'll pay ten percent of wholesale value." That was the same as 5 percent of retail, which meant they were offering about $22,550 reward for the stuff. At least now they were in the ball game.

Four hours later, at three that afternoon, I met with my first money snitch. I can't name him, like I can't name most of the others; his life would be worth nothing.

"It's buried in Old Man Black's backyard in Compton," he said. "It's close to a fruit tree, an old tree which I don't think they've watered in seven years so it's not bearing. It's easy to find."

"Why is it easy?" I said.

He said, "It's the only tree in the old man's backyard." He could have spared me the history.

Twice I had kicked in the old man's back door, but for this I needed something more. I needed an excuse to get into that backyard and dig. So I made a deal with Smokey Stover, who is a narcotics sergeant in the Compton PD. We stiffed in a hype to the pad, and he made a buy. The hype came out, and he went for a search warrant.

Then I called in the marines. I borrowed a metal detector from Camp Pendleton that detects five feet down. I got two Compton Fire Department units for their floodlights. And we went in with a warrant and secured the place, we lighted up that backyard like Dodger Stadium, and we went to work.

Old Man Black was not home when we moved in, just some young people not involved. But he came home in the middle of the action, and he said, "Hello, Mr. Franklin, what are you doing in my home again tonight?"

I said, "Maybe I'll tell you in a little while."

A few minutes later we found a plain cloth jewelry bag, no protection for the stuff at all, buried a few inches under the ground beside that nonbearing fruit tree. The jewelry in the bag counted out to $84,360 of Tiffany loot.

I went in and dumped the jewelry in front of Old Man Black, and we cuffed him, took him in and booked him.

We couldn't get a filing!

The DA in Compton said, first, he couldn't justify our taking a metal detector into the yard to look for narcotics, which is what we had a search warrant for. And second, Old Man Black had a lot of thieves coming and going there all the time, and anybody could have buried that stuff in his backyard.

For years people had been hollering against guilt by association, but this DA had discovered a new legal principle to help keep criminals on the street: exoneration by association. Know enough thieves, and nobody can touch you.

The insurance people paid off the snitch, and right away everybody was trying to get some of the action. The word was out that you turned in Tiffany jewelry, you got paid for it.

Primesburger's guys at LASO Firestone got the next deal. On August 27, nine months after the Tiffany robbery, they got a call, and three of their guys met somebody—I don't know who—at Rosecrans Avenue and Long Beach Boulevard in Compton, and the guy handed over 120 pieces of Tiffany jewelry worth $110,000.

I got the third call. The guy said, "I got what's left of the Tiffany stuff, and for the promise of no questions asked I'll meet you on a street corner and give it to you."

"Okay," I said, "no questions asked."

He said, "And no bust. Don't bring nobody else with you, I don't want to be busted on the spot."

I said, "Okay, no bust."

He told me the street corner and the time, and I went down, and there stood Old Man Black, the son of a bitch! He laid the jewelry on me, almost $100,000 worth, and I couldn't even ask him a question.

"You old son of a bitch, you!" I said. "I'm still going to arrest you for something." And I took the stuff, I went my way, and he went his way. But I never did arrest him again for anything, and I never will because I just don't give a damn anymore.

What he gave me wasn't the rest of the loot, like he promised. There is still more than $100,000 in Tiffany jewelry down in that Compton-South LA area, and somebody knows where it is. I don't.

We took Truman, Jr., and Wilson Black into court and we convicted both of them, which makes six out of six. Truman, Jr., got fifteen to life, and Judge Ewald gave Wilson 180 days' psychiatric study at Chino, and that's the total time he served.

The judge's theory was that this young man, twenty years old when he was arrested, deserved leniency because maybe he had been misguided and misled by the others involved.

My theory is that anybody that old is old enough to know the difference between right and wrong, and anybody smart enough to hide out for six months doesn't need a psychiatrist—he needs a prison cell to teach him a lesson if that's possible.

14

The Comstock Lode—Part I

IN MY twenty years of police work the Tiffany case was the one that forced me to think at the lowest gutter level, and the Red Velvet Gang was my most dangerous assignment. But the ski-mask bandits put up the biggest battle of wits; those guys were so clever that they are now being imitated all over the country and all over TV. They should get residuals. And for a little while there I was working on all three of these cases at the same time.

The ski-mask bandits made their first hit in June, 1973. In the next eleven months they ripped off $1,200,000 in cash and diamond jewelry in Beverly Hills and West LA. They never did stupid things, like the Tiffany bandits, and every job was very carefully cased and planned. They always knew exactly what they were after.

They wore ski masks so nobody could identify them, which is how they got their name. They always wore socks on their hands; they never left one fingerprint in eighteen jobs. They wore socks on their feet, no shoes, so they moved quietly and left no tracks. Many times they dismantled the telephone, so people couldn't call for help. They knew how to bypass burglar alarms, so they took every victim by complete surprise. And their MO never varied: They'd break into a house or apartment early in the morning, they'd wake the people up at gunpoint, and they'd take what they wanted.

What they wanted was cash and diamond jewelry, especially diamond jewelry. Nothing else. Many times it was a specific diamond they were after. They were very particular about this; they sneered at $3,000 watches unless the watch had diamonds on it. This discrimination was their trademark, and there was a reason for it, which we found out eventually.

The morning after Bruce Campbell and Ed Zenter and the guys busted me out of the Red Velvet Gang, first thing I went over to Pascal's on Doheny to get my hair cut, like Chief Cork had ordered. That's where he gets his hair cut too; a lot of us in the department go to Pascal.

I went in, and Pascal put down his *Playboy* magazine, got up from the chair and said, "You're late."

I hadn't talked to him or made any appointment, so I said, "What do you mean, I'm late?"

"The chief was in here earlier," he said, "and he made an appointment for you."

So I got my hair trimmed, and when I went back to the station, Cork says, "Okay, now that you look respectable enough to work here, I got a job for you and Bruce. Get these goddamned ski-mask bandits!"

They had already made three hits, and in fact, that same night they made a fourth. Bruce and I talked it over, and we decided we'd just start at the beginning and go back and recheck all the victims and see if we could spot something that had been missed.

Henry Witt was the first victim, so we started with him. Henry is a contractor who builds big shopping centers and then turns them over to a food chain or somebody like that to operate. He has a big house up on Rexford, and they got in there through a dog door at four o'clock in the morning and took a $25,000 diamond ring and some more stuff for a total of almost $28,000. So we started talking to Henry and his wife, Jeanne, and right away we picked up some interesting things.

"He passed up a lot of valuable stuff," Henry said.

"Like what?" Bruce said.

Henry showed us some jewelry trays the guy had gone through, and he had left most of what was there, very expensive stuff.

"He took it out and looked at it, and he put nearly all of it back," Jeanne said. "Now why would he do that?"

That's what I was wondering. But I couldn't think of an answer.

"He kept asking for my big ring," Jeanne said. "That's the twenty-five-thousand-dollar ring that goes with my wedding band. He took that, too."

"That's your biggest ring?" I said.

She said yes, but Henry put in, "It's curious, I hadn't thought of it until just now, but I had a bigger ring until just a few days ago. It's a ring I ordered out from Harry Winston, the New York jeweler, just on approval. They priced it at one hundred thousand dollars."

I said, "What happened to it?"

"Oh," he said, "I had it appraised here, and apparently it wasn't worth that much. At least the appraisal discouraged me. The Winston man tried to get me to keep it another week, but I sent it back."

Another week, and that $100,000 diamond ring would not have been the one the ski-mask bandits barely missed. For a time there we wondered if the Winston salesman in New York was pulling something, but we cleared him.

What might have happened, the only way we could figure it, was that Henry and Jeanne had been out to dinner a couple of nights before the robbery at Sneaky Pete's in West Hollywood, her wearing the $25,000 ring, and the ski-mask bandits had spotted it then and maybe trailed them home to find out where they lived. There had to be some way they knew about her big ring, and our guess turned out to be their MO.

Henry and Jeanne saw only one guy, but he said to them, "Just be quiet and nobody will get hurt. If you make any noise, my partner will take care of your boy."

But that couldn't be right because they had the door to the kid's room closed and there was a big Doberman in there. It looked like the guy just pretended he had a partner.

At least Henry could laugh about it. "I got that big vicious dog to protect us," he said. "We're all afraid of it, and it sleeps all through the robbery."

Then he began to talk about how the guy moved around like an athlete or a dancer, very agile and graceful, and Jeanne said how he talked with some sibilance and a tinge of a New York accent, and all of a sudden Bruce and I looked at each other and at the same time we both said, "Hut!"

Hut is Hutton Salisbury, a cat burglar we busted in Beverly Hills back in 1967, when we had a big series of hillside rip-offs. He always worked with a partner we busted with him, a guy named Bart McBroom who got to be known as Comstock because he came from that part of Nevada. Comstock and Hut, they always worked together, and they ripped off so much sugar that everybody in the underworld called them C & H.

Back in the 1960s C & H gave us a lot of trouble. They pulled burglaries almost every night. We'd stake out one place, and they'd hit two doors down the street; it was uncanny. The night we got them it was dense fog, and Jack Egger, who is now a captain, rounded a corner of the house and came face to face with Comstock. Comstock went over a low retaining wall, and Jack fired his shotgun at him but missed. Comstock fell about a hundred feet down a hillside and got knocked out for about ten minutes, but we couldn't find him in the fog. But we nabbed Hut, and we got Comstock the next day.

Both of them had committed crimes all over the map. Comstock pulled 300 jobs in Miami, and all they could get him on was trespass; they forgot to advise him of his constitutional rights.

Comstock is a likable, friendly guy and one of the world's best con artists. He and Hut pulled several burglaries down around Palm Springs; one that they probably did was a burglary at the home of the former President, Dwight Eisenhower, when he was still alive. That one still isn't solved, but around that time Sergeant Joe Jones of the Palm Springs Police Department spotted Comstock in Palm Springs, which was a violation of his parole. Joe busted him for that, but he couldn't file on him for burglary without evidence.

Comstock offered him a deal; he'd try to get some of the stuff back. And Joe bought it. So Comstock spent a couple of weeks living it up at government expense in Palm Springs.

Finally, he told Joe, "I'm sorry, it's out of my reach; it's in South America. There's nothing I can do about it."

And there was nothing Joe could do. He had made a promise, and he kept it. He couldn't prove that Comstock hadn't kept his part of the deal, so he had to drop it.

Later Comstock pulled the same trick on Sergeant Tom Rogers of LAPD West LA Division. By then Comstock was in Folsom Prison, and he conned Tom into thinking he could get back some LA jewelry that he said had been fenced in Miami. So Tom got him out of prison and took him to Miami for two weeks of wining and dining at the taxpayers' expense. And at the end of two weeks it was the same story: The stuff was out of reach. Tom is one of the best cops around, but Comstock can con the best.

So now we thought C & H were back in our midst in Beverly Hills, except this time they were pulling gun robberies instead of cat burglaries. But the guy that hit Henry Witt's place was alone, it looked like, so if he was Hut, where was Comstock?

The second case clued us that C & H were working

together again. David and Sophie Simon, retired people who lived in an apartment on South Reeves, on the second floor, went to lunch at Nate-n-Al's on Beverly Drive, and Sophie was wearing a 12-carat diamond ring worth about $18,000.

At five o'clock in the afternoon a guy who looked like Comstock followed the Simons into the building where they lived, went into the garage for no reason and knocked on doors asking for people who didn't live there.

At five o'clock the next morning a guy who looked like Hut climbed an extension ladder to the Simons' bathroom window, went into their bedroom and woke them up. He wanted Sophie's dinner ring. "I don't have a dinner ring," she said.

"You're lying," the guy said. "You went out for lunch yesterday at Nate-n-Al's and you wore it." So she gave it to him, and he left.

I never did find out where that big ladder came from until after we had busted C & H and sent them back to prison. Then I visited them out at Chino prison, and Hut said. "I got it about a mile away, on Olympic."

They carried that damned ladder all the way to the job, ducking down alleys and popping into bushes whenever a car came along.

They hit the Charles Sandoval home in Bel Air—they are people who own a bunch of factories down in Mississippi— and they walked away with $33,000. They bypassed the burglar alarm system some way LAPD never could figure— they got in by lifting a sliding door off its track—and Hut scared poor Mildred Sandoval half to death when he came out from behind some draperies while she was watching TV.

"He came walking right out of the refrigerator," she said. It just looked that way, of course, but I think she was more impressed with that than with the fact she was out $33,000 in jewels.

The day Bruce and I began our investigation they ripped

off Harmon Bellows in Beverly Hills for about $23,500. Harmon is an attorney who used to practice criminal law until he got disgusted with it and went into corporate law, and he has a very elaborate home up in Trousdale. He was planning a trip to Hawaii in a day or two, for which he had pulled $5,500 in cash out of the bank and put it on his bureau dresser; Harmon likes to have a pocketful of money when he travels.

About two o'clock in the morning he couldn't sleep, so he got up, turned off the burglar alarm system and went into a den to watch TV.

He fell asleep in there. About four thirty he woke up, and a guy in a ski mask was holding a gun on him. He made Harmon go back into the bedroom and wake up Stephanie. They went into the dressing room, where she keeps her jewelry, and she pulled out some pearls.

"No, I don't want that," he said, "just diamonds. I want the big diamond ring."

She said, "I don't have it."

"You're lying," he said. "You've been seen wearing it."

"Yes," she said, "but I took it back and put it in the vault at the bank."

She was conning him, but it worked. The guy pulled open one drawer and took some valuable jewelry out of it, but he didn't open the next drawer. That's where the $50,000 ring was.

"You shouldn't pull that kind of stuff," I told Stephanie. "If he had pulled out that drawer and found it, he might have got mad." Hut was always as polite as a waiter truckling for a big tip; he would hold a gun on a guy but always call him "sir."

"How did you get into my house?" Harmon Bellows asked him.

"Well, sir," he said, "I came through the sliding door in the den. Your door was open about six inches, and to set your alarm, you have to have all the doors closed." He knew a lot about alarms, but he didn't really know that one; he was just lucky: Harmon's door could be open that much and the alarm still on but not triggered—it was a new system. The reason it didn't trigger this time was that Harmon had turned the system off.

After he got what he wanted, Hut told Harmon and Stephanie to stay in bed, and he split. Harmon waited about two minutes and started to get up to phone the police. The guy stuck his head back in and said, "Sir, I said stay in bed. Don't get up."

What happened was Comstock was outside as a lookout, and when he saw Hut coming out, he took off up the road. He ran up a steep bank next to where Harry Karl and Debbie Reynolds used to live and on over into LA, where their car was parked. When Hut looked around outside and didn't see Comstock, he thought his partner had gone inside, so he went back in to check.

That parking in LA was another of their trademarks that we didn't know about until we busted them. They always parked in LA because of the Beverly Hills overnight parking ordinance, and they walked to their jobs. That made it harder for us to catch them because we never found their cars while they were on a job.

So now it was July, they'd pulled four jobs in a month, and we were starting to work on it. But they kept pulling jobs, and we got nowhere. We found where they were living without much trouble, we identified their associates; but we couldn't catch them on a job, and we couldn't get physical evidence for a conviction. It was frustrating.

They were living in an apartment on Hacienda Place in West Hollywood, C & H and Comstock's girlfriend, a United Air Lines stewardess named Sandy Showers. There was another guy in the group, Bill Ringer, who had another apartment there; he had been Sandy's boyfriend until she switched over to Comstock.

That apartment was an interesting place. It was leased by

a master burglar, Sean Hanratty, who was in prison while I was working undercover in the Red Velvet Gang. Everything in Hanratty's apartment was owned by thieves, and everybody who lived in that apartment was a thief. When one guy went to prison, he just sold his stuff to another crook that was moving in, and Hanratty collected the rent. When we finally busted C & H, almost everything they had in the apartment, which was nicely furnished, they had bought from Hanratty, and almost every item was on somebody's hot list.

Comstock liked the place because it was cheap. After the bust I said, "Why the hell do you come back into a hot area where you're well known, where by the law of averages if you stay with it you're going to get caught?"

And he said, "Where else are you going to find a nice place like this for a hundred twenty-five a month?"

But even Comstock didn't know that most of his furniture and stuff was stolen. He got very annoyed with Hanratty about that, like when I showed him a crime report that his typewriter had been stolen in Santa Barbara.

"Jesus Christ, Lynn!" he said. "I never stole *nothing* from Santa Barbara. And I don't steal typewriters; that's bush league. I *bought* that typewriter from Sean Hanratty!"

Comstock's biggest problem was that he was greedy, and like all con-artists, he conned himself into thinking he wouldn't get caught. If he and Hut had been willing to pull half a dozen jobs in Beverly Hills and then move on to New York or Miami or wherever and keep moving on, they'd probably still be running. But the pickings in Beverly Hills were too easy, and he conned himself into thinking he could keep it up forever, even though Beverly Hills was the only place he had ever failed heavy, back in 1967.

And he was lazy. Most criminals are lazy, and Comstock, being one of the brightest, was also one of the laziest.

"Comstock is too damned lazy to get a job and go to work," Sandy Showers told me later. "He'll lay in the bushes for hours, waiting to move in and rip somebody off, but he wouldn't get up in the morning and go punch a clock. He sleeps all day."

I said, "He sleeps all day? He's out at night? What about your sex life?"

And she said, very strong and frustrated, "He *sleeps* all the time!" In the long run all that sleeping helped convict him; he'd have been safer to overdo sex.

Probably it's too bad Comstock didn't have more education. He quit in the tenth grade, and he finally got a high school diploma in prison. He never learned any trade or craft except stealing. I'm no sociologist, I don't want to be, and I'll never pretend to be; but some of the guys I've handled, like Comstock and Len Swinger, I'll always wonder about what they might have been.

Comstock's brilliance was what kept us from catching the ski-mask bandits until Mother's Day of 1974. He was the leader, like Ben Colt in the Red Velvet Gang, and the tactics and the MO were all his.

They played games with cars. Even back in 1967 they were so tail-conscious that there was no way to follow them in cars. But now they had figured out ways to use cars like the old shell game; they shuffled them around so fast they dazzled pursuit.

They had a Cadillac, a Datsun, a dune buggy and a motorcycle at their disposal. Comstock would come out and take the Cadillac out of the carport and drive away. Then Sandy Showers would pull away in the Datsun, which was hers, and she'd lose pursuit and come back with Comstock on foot, or on the motorcycle, or in a white Volkswagen which belonged to Bill Ringer's sister, Pearl, and then Ringer would drive up in the Cad, and Hut would take it out, and he'd come back in the dune buggy, which we hadn't even noticed leaving. It was like a chess game; the combinations were up in the billions.

About the only thing we had going for us at this time was United Air Lines, which kept us informed about every flight Sandy was assigned to. This was important because she drove them to all their jobs, and if she was only driving out to the airport to go to work, we could relax.

And the hits kept coming. In September they hit Cartan Vittorio's seventeenth-floor penthouse for more than $100,000. Pearl Ringer had fingered Vittorio, who is one of the biggest civic and society guys in LA; she managed to meet him at the Greek Theater. Pearl was a movie-struck little gal who would lay with anybody while waiting for her big break, and meanwhile, she did this kind of thing on the side.

How they did it, they got into the fire-escape well which went all the way to the roof. From there Comstock dropped Hut down to the penthouse patio on a rope; I found his foot scratches where he came down the wall. And Hut just walked in through the patio sliding glass doors, which nobody on the seventeenth floor bothered to lock. They should have, because about the same time some cat burglars went to the roof of another building on Wilshire and cleaned out nine floors by working down. Altitude is not protection.

They did two other high-rise jobs, both in LA, one where they picked up $75,000 in a fifteenth-floor penthouse and another where they got into the seventeenth-story penthouse of a doctor, Andre Weir, but got only about $6,000.

Comstock got the high-rise idea from watching a "human fly" movie being made in Phoenix. They had a stunt man climb the outside of some fifteen- or eighteen-story building there and supposedly go in and rip off something, and Comstock happened by and watched while they filmed it. A month later he went back and did the same thing for real at the same building; he ripped off eight places. Hut was with him in the car as a lookout, and also Bill Ringer's brother, Bob, who is now in law school studying how to get away with legal rip-offs and who will probably be a judge someday.

They hit Sid Sidonis in Beverly Hills two nights after he

bought his wife, Laura, a new Rolls-Royce. Both Sid and Laura are theatrical agents, and she is such a jeweled little flirt that she is known around town as Diamond Lil. C & H were wheeling down Beverly Drive in their Cadillac, and suddenly there was Diamond Lil in her brand-new Rolls, and they were waving and smiling at each other, and that $25,000 diamond of hers was blinding our boys.

She put the Rolls in a parking lot, and Comstock strolled in and read the new car sticker on the inside of the windshield, from which he got DMV directions to the scene of the robbery.

Hut always knew where he was anyway. During the robbery he picked up Laura's purse and cracked, "If it's Gucci, this must be Beverly Hills."

Comstock knew we were working him, and he was always trying to find out what we were up to. One day he had the nerve to drop into the station. He talked to Captain Jack Egger, the same guy who shot at him in the fog seven years before, and Jack recognized him but he didn't recognize Jack.

After some casual good-citizen-type chatter Comstock said, "I guess you got a real problem with those ski-mask guys."

Jack said, "Yeah, but don't worry, we'll bust them any time now. We know who it is, a couple of fags out in Santa Monica, and we're working them day and night."

From that Comstock felt a little easier, so Jack managed to con the great con man.

C & H got a better view of Beverly Hills than you can get from the Gray Line sightseeing bus. They saw some of the most beautiful asses in town, stark naked.

One of them belongs to Elizabeth Orange. She and her husband, Bert, had just come home from a late-dinner party and they were getting ready for bed. C & H and Bill Ringer were outside the bedroom in the bushes, watching them.

"Boy, that Elizabeth Orange has a body!" Comstock told

me later. "Everybody wanted to rush right in right then. I had to tell them no. I want no panic with naked women running around. I made them wait until the nighties were on; then we went in and ripped them off."

They got $17,000 in jewelry, $2,500 in cash, and $10,000 in foreign currency, Swiss, French, English and Italian. They also got a five-pound bag of marijuana that Bert Orange didn't mention when he reported the loss.

At the trial I told Bert about it, and he looked funny. I said, "It doesn't matter to me, but they may bring it up, and you ought to be prepared. It's your problem." But it never came up.

Jill Jacklin reacted to Hut like almost every woman did; the guy must be some kind of sex symbol. Her husband, Jerry, is a real estate broker, Jill has a fantastic figure from riding horses all the time, and they both sleep in the nude.

When they woke up under the gun and Hut told Jerry to get out of the bed and get the jewelry, Jerry said, "I don't have any clothes on." And he rolled over to Jill and said, "You get it for him, honey."

So Jill got out of bed, wearing nothing but her skin. She grabbed a pillow to hold in front of her. At the trial she said, "It was a very small pillow," and the courtroom broke up.

She went into her dressing room where the jewelry was, and Hut followed her, and she put a robe on.

"I turned around to him," she said, "and he's in the room right next to me, not a foot away, and I looked in his eyes. He had the most beautiful blue eyes I ever saw."

We got four IDs on Hut just from his beautiful blue eyes, but that one impressed the jury the most.

Judy Billingford Rojas never got a chance to impress the jury. She was a good-looking divorcée with a couple of kids, the heiress to a Midwestern machinery fortune, and she lived in a big house up on Summit Drive.

The night she got hit she had a boyfriend visiting her, a lawyer from Minneapolis, and they went out to Trader

Vic's for dinner. They came back to Summit Drive and hopped into bed together, and that was where Hut found them. He had trouble getting enough of their attention so he could rob them of $81,000; in fact, he had to pull them apart physically.

After Hut got their attention, Judy said, "Can I get something on?"

Hut said okay, and she got out of bed and went to her dressing room for a robe. By this time the scene must have looked to Hut like a TV rerun.

Between the robbery and the time several months later that I got Judy down to county jail for a lineup, she had married a very prominent California congressman. And he came down to the jail with her.

She pulled me over to the side and said, "Lynn, *please!* You *know* I can't identify anybody, and you know *why.*"

In circumstances like that, all you can do is salute the lady and say adios. We lost a witness.

By December 13 we had had nine ski-mask robberies in six months, and I was getting as impatient as the bridegroom the night before the wedding. What we were doing, which was traditional police tactics, wasn't working.

"What I want," I told Chief Cork, "is to activate SET." SET is our Special Enforcement Team, a predecessor to the SWAT teams that have popped up recently. In Beverly Hills SET is put together only under special circumstances; it is not a permanent organization.

But SET costs money because there are special expenses and overtime, it takes people off their regular duties, and it is about as hard to get aloft as the famous lead balloon unless you have a real emergency. I couldn't convince anybody that we had a real emergency.

Five months and half a million dollars' worth of ski-mask rip-offs later, we got what anybody could see was an emergency. A murder.

A guy wearing a ski mask got into a fifteenth-floor apartment on Wilshire Boulevard, in LAPD territory, and gagged an elderly man, Barrett Rogers, with one of his wife's stockings. The commotion woke up their son, Kent. He tried to rush the guy, and the guy shot him three times, killing him.

It is a question whether the killer was Hut, because the business with the stocking gag did not follow my ski-mask bandits' MO. And the loot was only $700, which those guys wouldn't have bothered with. We never got an ID on the killer because of the ski mask, but LAPD filed on Hut anyway. The case is still pending, and I doubt that it will ever be solved.

But the murder jolted the higher-ups, five months too late. Ed Zenter and Bruce Campbell and Lee Tracy and some of the guys were offering to work a SET team without pay, on their own time, and finally, Chief Cork agreed.

Zenter was the commander of SET, and Tracy the field commander. They both were sergeants, and it probably seems funny to an outsider that I was put in charge, but we didn't operate strictly by rank in the Beverly Hills department. If a guy was experienced and it was his case, he knew the most about it, he was the boss. We found it worked.

So Zenter and Tracy and I made a plan, and Cork said, "What are you going to do?"

"We're going to set up a command post right where they live," I said. "We're going to watch those sons of bitches, and we're going to get them!"

Cork said, "Look, we've all had experience with them. You can't follow those guys. You cannot tail them."

He was right; nobody had ever been able to tail them— they were too smart. LAPD worked them for two months with ground units and helicopters, and they got absolutely zero. But LAPD was using a paid snitch in the building on Hacienda, and they didn't know that the snitch was playing a double game. Every time they'd back off C & H knew it, and they'd pull another job.

So I said to Cork, "The way I'm going to tail them, you

can tail them. If they go away, the bird always comes home. We'll keep a loose tail, and if we lose them, don't worry. If they pull a job, we'll take them when they come back."

"When they come back, they never come back with anything," Cork said. "They get rid of it first. You know that as well as I. What are you going to have then?"

I said, "I'm going to have the son of a bitch that pulled the job!"

"But they're not going to tell you the time of day," he said. "You can't break them down."

"Cork," I said, "I've broke down people a hell of a lot tougher than C & H. You can bet your ass I'll get them!"

That was when he gave a final okay, and we put the team together. LAPD turned what they had over to me, and I got their best people too: Tom Rogers from West LA and Charlie Ross and Del Baker from LAPD Criminal Conspiracy. And from Beverly Hills we had Captain Wayne Rutherford, Captain Jack Egger, Lieutenant Ed Greene, and Zenter and Tracy and Campbell and me, plus now and then another guy.

Cork gave me $78 from the slush fund for a week's rent, and I checked into the Holloway Motel across Holloway Drive from the apartment. I used my own name, but I said I was from Jackson, Mississippi; I sound like it anyway. My suitcases were full of surveillance gear, and I got a room where the bathroom window looked directly across the street into the sun deck of their apartment and beyond that a double window into the bedroom. The shade was pulled most of the time, but you could see the bedroom light turned off and on, and you could see activity out on the sun deck, which had latticework across the front.

We replaced the window screen with a one-way glass that looked like a screen; we could see out, but nobody could see in. The guy on watch had to put the toilet seat down and sit on it to look out the window; after several hours of sitting there, that seat got mighty hard, and we wore out two or three pillows before the job was done. But that was the only window in LA that had the view we needed, and it didn't matter if the accommodations didn't compare with the Hilton.

Their sun deck had a built-in ladder up to the flat roof, and two or three times we saw Comstock or Hut climb up there and look around, checking the neighborhood for police activity.

And every night Comstock would come out and walk his German shepherd for one purpose only, to look the situation over. He was watching traffic, who was parked where, any movement that was going on. That was the most walked dog in the neighborhood.

One night he stopped just below our window and stood there for a couple of minutes, looking up. Later he told me he wondered if police were watching him out that window, and he thought of waving but decided it was too risky.

Sandy Showers we'd see going in and out, getting into the Datsun to go on a flight, or sometimes Comstock would drive her to the airport in the Cadillac. We always knew when she was leaving and when she'd be back.

One evening I took a nap for a couple of hours, leaving Lieutenant Chuck Mennen on duty at the window. When I came back, I could see Comstock out there walking his dog, but Chuck wasn't paying any attention; he was watching a car parked right below us. I looked down, and here was a guy and a gal screwing in the car -and Chuck couldn't see anything else.

They finished their fun, lighted up cigarettes and started talking, and Comstock went back inside the apartment, so I went out and walked up to the car. I leaned in, showed my badge and said, "Look, you people, I'm a police officer and we're running a surveillance here, and you're distracting my guys so they're not paying attention. I don't mind you having a little fun, but get the hell out of here, will you?"

The guy got mad, but the girl just laughed. She was sitting there with her skirt still pulled up so her crotch showed, and her blouse was unbuttoned, and she had very big tits hanging out, and she didn't even bother to cover up. She just laughed, and the guy muttered something and kicked the engine over, and they split. She gave me a little wave as they went.

A lot of women are funny that way; if they know you're a cop or if you're wearing a uniform, any kind of uniform, it's like you're just an object, you don't exist. I noticed that when I first got out of the army and I was a milkman for about six months before I got to farming strawberries. I'd walk into a kitchen to deliver some milk, and the gal would be sitting there drinking coffee and all exposed in a nightie or something, and she wouldn't cover up or pay any attention to me. Just like the girl in the car.

The show wasn't always as good as that time, but there was always something going on. One night a guy wearing a cowboy outfit pulled up in a Buick and went into C & H's apartment. We ran the Buick license, and it came back to Joe Jones, Palm Springs. It was Sergeant Joe Jones, the guy we knew that Comstock had conned, and he was in LA to attend a special surveillance course; he was concerned about how Comstock was getting along. So Comstock invited him over for dinner. He said Sandy was a great cook, which I never had the chance to find out.

Comstock and Joe came down and got into the dune buggy and drove off. I had a unit follow them, and they went down off Santa Monica Boulevard and looked over a couple of trucks that C & H had; they were parked there. The trucks were a front they used; they worked them now and then for a guy named Howard Stanton up near Fresno, in the San Joaquin. Stanton had got himself involved in this thing in an odd way that we only found out about later, during the trial. But this night Comstock was showing Joe Jones the trucks and conning him some more, making him believe that's how he and Hut made a living.

The original plan was to continue the surveillance for about thirty days. They usually hit about every two weeks, so in a month we ought to get one chance at them for sure.

But after the first week I had a hell of a time getting the okay to continue. It wasn't just the $78 rent; it was more the overtime. Cork didn't like it, but we got another week.

About the tenth night activity started to pick up. They shuffled those cars around like corns on a bingo board. They'd take the dune buggy out, leave it somewhere, come back in the Datsun, park it and get in the Cadillac, drive it around the corner and park it again, any crazy thing just to see if anybody was tailing them.

On the thirteenth night the activity really picked up, and we all felt this had to be it. We alerted West Hollywood LASO, because this is their territory, that we might need help at any time.

About eleven o'clock Comstock got in the Datsun and drove off, and we ordered a ground unit to follow him. He drove around in a five-mile circle and finally got into a right-turn-only pocket on Santa Monica. The unit was right behind him. When the light changed, Comstock went straight ahead, looking in his rearview mirror to see if anybody else broke the law, which would be the giveaway.

All our guy could do was turn right, radio the information, whip a U and try to fall in behind again. Comstock wandered around some more, and finally, when he got about a mile south of Beverly Hills, we ordered the unit to drop off. Better to lose him than get burned.

A little after midnight Sandy came out with Hut and Bill Ringer, and they went off in the Datsun. She came back a little later alone, turned off the lights and went to bed.

About two o'clock in the morning the lights came on again. She came out, got in the Cadillac, circled the block, then made a larger circle of about eight blocks to come back by the apartment. And now Hut and Ringer were in the Cad with her.

She headed west through Beverly Hills to Westwood, being very careful to obey all the traffic rules. At Westwood Boulevard she made a right, and after one block she made another right onto Massachusetts Avenue. And she just disappeared. Four units were tailing her, and they couldn't find a trace.

About an hour later Sandy returned to the apartment in the Cadillac, parked it in the carport, went in and went to bed again.

Everything was quiet until a little after five o'clock, when the call came on the radio: The ski-mask bandits had just pulled a job on Summit Drive, at the home of an attorney named Jonathan St. Cloud. They got $24,600 in diamond jewelry, plus some cash.

We deployed our units to cover every approach, and we waited. About forty-five minutes later Lee Tracy radioed from his post up on Fountain Avenue, "The Datsun is coming up behind me right now. He's stopping almost parallel to me. It's Comstock driving, Hut and Ringer with him. No, wait, Ringer's getting out. He's barefoot. He's heading on foot down Hacienda. The Datsun is now southbound on Hacienda."

Zenter stayed with the radio. Campbell and I got out to the street. The Datsun pulled up to the stop sign at Holloway, and there was only one guy in it now, Comstock.

Campbell and I moved in from both sides, and Campbell laid a magnum on him and said, "If you move, Comstock, I'll blow your goddamned head off!"

Comstock told me later that he couldn't remember if his foot was on the brake or the gas pedal. He said, "The guy is standing there telling me he's going to kill me if the car rolls at all, and I want to put my foot down to keep it at a standstill, and I'm thinking if it's the gas pedal, the car is going to move forward, and he's going to kill me."

I said, "That's exactly what Bruce was going to do. He would have killed you."

"Well," he said, "I put my foot down, and God was with me, it was the brake."

At the same time we were busting Comstock, Lee Tracy rolled up alongside Ringer a block away and hit his brakes. Ringer told me later he didn't think it was a police car until Lee rolled out and pumped a shell into his shotgun and said, "Freeze, motherfucker, or I'll blow your head off!"

We had Comstock and Ringer, and Sandy was in the apartment, but Hut got away. He had dropped out of the Datsun somewhere between Fountain and Holloway.

When Campbell and I had grabbed Comstock, Zenter was watching us, and he put out the call, and all hell broke loose.

"My God, it sounded like the Normandy invasion," Hut told me afterward. "Units must have been rolling in from every direction. I took off. I went between buildings and over fences; all the way up to Sunset I never stopped running. I was so scared I ran right into the traffic on Sunset and almost got knocked over by a sheriff's car rolling in at about sixty."

Meanwhile, Bruce jerked Comstock out of the Datsun and spread-eagled him over the car, and what was dangling out of his right hip pocket was a ski mask with several little Italian pine needles sticking in it.

When we checked out the St. Cloud place, we found the Italian pine tree the needles came from. Comstock had been standing under it, and those needles helped prove it in court.

And in his front pocket we found something else: a single teardrop diamond earring. It was the only piece of jewelry on any of them; they had got rid of the rest of the stuff before heading back to the roost, but that one earring had been overlooked.

We went over to C & H's pad, and it had iron bars on the door. Bruce and I took turns kicking doors. I took one look at those bars and said, "Bruce, it's your turn."

And the son of a gun actually tried to kick those bars. He was lucky he didn't break a foot. We were yelling, "Police officers! Open the door!" And the German shepherd inside was barking its head off, and finally Sandy cracked the door on the chain. We told her to secure the dog, so she locked it in the bathroom, and then she opened the door, and we cuffed her.

We didn't search the place, not right then. We got a warrant, which took six hours, and then we searched.

But while we were in there, the phone rang, and Zenter grabbed for it. He had been trying to get even with me ever since I answered the phone and caught a guy the night we got into that crazy chase in the Purple Phantom convertible. So this time he beat me to it, and he said, "Yeah?"

And the guy on the other end said, "It's junk. It's costume. It's no good." It was the receiver C & H had just laid the St. Cloud jewelry on before they came home.

Ed caught on real fast and said, "Well, bring it back."

"All right, I'll bring it over," the guy said.

"How soon?" Ed said.

The guy said, "I'll be there in five minutes."

"Okay," Ed said. "We'll meet you on Holloway."

He hung up, and I said, "Get all the police units out of here! Get *everything* out of here!"

Everybody was screaming at everybody else and moving cars out, and this took a few minutes, and Campbell ran down to move the Datsun, which was still standing where we had stopped it in the middle of the street. He backed it into the carport, and he was just stepping out when another car drove up to the curb and stopped, and a heavyset gray-haired old guy got out.

The old guy took one look at Campbell, the walking image of a cop, and he got back in his car quick and took off. We put the units on him, and Lee Tracy and Dave Griffey stopped him a couple of blocks away.

"What are you doing up here?" Lee said.

The old guy said, "I just came up for a walk."

"Well, then," Lee said, "why didn't you go for a walk?"

"I changed my mind," he said.

They talked a little more, and finally, Dave opened up the glove compartment of the car, and in it was a bag containing the $24,600 worth of jewelry that had just been ripped off at St. Cloud's.

It was all there except for one piece, the mate to the teardrop diamond earring we found in Comstock's pocket. Those earrings, we found later, had been specially designed for St. Cloud's wife, Joy, by a jeweler in New York, and they were unique. There was not another earring in the whole world that matched those.

This was a bigger jackpot than we ever expected. It was the first recovery of any jewels after eleven months and eighteen robberies totaling $1,200,000, and we had the evidence to tie it all to C & H.

The old guy's name is Jerry Chesterfield, he is a retired jeweler and a diamond expert, and as soon as we found the jewels, he changed his story about wanting to take a walk.

Now the story was that he had just within the hour picked the stuff up from a guy named Jack Platte for appraisal, but it was all junk costume jewelry, and he was taking it back to Platte. He knew damned well that we knew Platte as a big-time receiver, and we were supposed to think that Platte was the fence for C & H. And we were also supposed to believe that this was a normal thing for a seventy-four-year-old retired jeweler to be doing between five and six o'clock on a Sunday morning.

And it wasn't just any ordinary Sunday; it was Mother's Day!

So we took Chesterfield in, and now we were looking for Hut. The next morning I got a call from a lawyer named Paul Black, from the office of the famous criminal lawyer Peter Tenner. I had known Paul from other cases, and he told me he was handling Sandy Showers' case.

"I'm in contact with somebody who's in contact with Hutton Salisbury," he said. "What's going to happen to him?"

I said, "Paul, it looks like he killed a guy. There's no doubt in my mind that he's responsible. He's on the run, and when we find him, we're going to kill the son of a bitch. That's exactly what's going to happen to him."

So Paul said, "I'll get back to you."

Ten minutes later he was back. "I'll make a deal with you, Lynn," he said. "You got a high bail on Sandy, and I doubt you want her that bad. If you'll drop her bail and let her hit the streets, I can arrange for Hut to surrender."

So I said, "I'll tell you what I'll do. I'm not going to let her hit the streets until I've got Hut. You bring him to me, and then I'll recommend a lower bail for Sandy."

"Okay," he said.

I got a warrant out for Hut, and two days later he walked into the station with his attorney, George Bancroft, who is also his cousin from San Francisco, and Bancroft handed the guy over to me.

So we had busted the whole gang; we had physical evidence; we even got the receiver; we had a solid case. The question now was whether we could get it through the goddamned courts.

15

The Comstock Lode—Part II

THE MORNING after the bust everybody wanted to get into the act and take a bow. Everybody figured we had a winner; it was a case to get famous on.

Sam Lord, out of the DA's office in Santa Monica, was in the Beverly Hills office at eight in the morning. I said, "What are you doing here?"

"I'm taking the ski-mask case," he said.

"The hell you are!" I said. I knew how that bastard handled his cases, and he wasn't half tough enough to suit me. "Gregg Marcus is handling this one," I said. "He's right here in this office."

"No," Sam said, "I'm taking it over."

He could pull that stuff on a lot of guys, but not on me. I picked up the phone and called Bob Wilson, Sam's boss in Santa Monica. "Bob," I said, "Sam Lord is over here wanting to take the ski-mask case. You'd better order him back to Santa Monica before I kick his balls off or something. Gregg Marcus is going to handle it."

"Is Sam there now?" Bob said.

"Yeah," I said, "he's right here."

"Let me talk to him."

I put Sam on, and he listened for a minute and hung up. "Gee, Lynn, I'm sorry," he said, "but I can't take the ski-mask case after all. I got a bigger one Bob wants me to handle in Santa Monica."

It was all right with me if he wanted to lie and put a face on it, as long as I got rid of him.

Gregg Marcus is a fighting son of a gun, but no deputy DA can cope with downtown. They would let him file on only five cases: St. Cloud, naturally, plus Jerry Jacklin, Dr. Andre Weir, Charles Sandoval and Sid Sidonis. It burned me up.

"How come only five?" I said to Gregg.

"Lynn," he said, "you know how it is. They just arbitrarily said five, no more. They're afraid that if we file on all eighteen, we might lose a few, and that would bring down the DA's percentage of convictions."

I said, "Goddamn his percentage! These people ought to be put away for as long as possible, and those bastards downtown are playing games with statistics! We can convict them on every case, and you know it!"

"Yeah," Gregg said, "but you forget one thing."

"What's that?"

"There's an election for DA every four years."

So because the boss wanted his percentage to look good, we had to go easy on C & H, which is not a way to protect society from criminals.

When we went to preliminary was the first time in my life I was thankful for a crowded calendar. They didn't want to pull a Beverly Hills judge off everything else for the two weeks we figured it would take, so they brought in Judge William Osborne, from Avalon over on Catalina Island. In my book this guy rates with guys like William Drake downtown, and Homer Garrott out in Compton, and Leo Freund here in Beverly Hills, and Laurence Rittenband out in Santa Monica, judges that are tough but fair and that know their law. There are some other good ones, too, but damned few of them. Judge Osborne is one of the few.

Almost the first thing that happened was that Hut's attorney, George Bancroft, wanted the judge to set a bail so Hut could get back on the street. Hut was charged with homicide in the Kent Rogers killing, and while that is technically bailable in California, as a practical matter it usually isn't because even lousy judges won't go for it.

Bancroft had the gall to claim that Hut had submitted voluntarily to a lie detector test for LAPD and that he had walked in and surrendered to me voluntarily, and all this proved he was a nice, trustworthy soul and the judge should set bail.

This was all lies. Hut had to be pressured to take the lie test, and surrendering to avoid getting killed didn't impress the judge as an act of charity. He wasn't conned. He just said, "No bail."

Bancroft and I were never going to get along anyway, not from the minute he walked in with Hut and surrendered him, because that's when I knew that in talking to Paul Black, I had really been talking to George Bancroft, who didn't have the guts to deal with me directly.

And Bancroft didn't like me because he had got the word from Paul Black that I was the guy who said we would kill his cousin. Then he started hassling my victims on the witness stand and trying to discredit them and me instead of trying to prove his client innocent, which was impossible, and after twenty years of that crap George Bancroft was one more shyster than I needed.

Finally, I cornered him out in the hallway during a recess, and I had Ed Zenter as a witness, and I said to Bancroft, "We go back into court, Bancroft, and you keep getting too personal and trying to drag me and my people through the mud, and after this court's over with, I'm going to take you down the alley by the power plant behind this courthouse, and I'm going to sweep that alley with the goddamned hair on your head."

And he said, "What are you talking about?"

I said, "I'm not pulling your leg. I'm not kidding you. That bullshit doesn't go. So knock it off, or I'll beat your goddamned eyes in."

"I'm going to talk to your chief," he said, very indignant.

"Be my guest," I said. "I'll take you over there and introduce you, or I'll give you a dime here and you can call him on the phone."

He turned to Zenter and he said, "Jesus Christ! I've never had anybody talk to me like this!"

And Zenter said, "Well, you'd better watch your step, or he'll probably do just what he said. He always does."

I had to put in another word. "You son of a bitch," I said, "you shouldn't be on this case. You're trying to defend a cousin; it's like a doctor operating on his own wife. You should get out of it unless you need the money so bad."

Bancroft went back in and talked to the other defense lawyers about filing a complaint, but I guess they told him to cool it because he did nothing. He stopped hassling my victims, and after the preliminary he backed off the case completely, and Hut got another lawyer.

It wasn't until after Hut was convicted that I found out how unethical Bancroft could be. Before Hut surrendered, Bancroft told him there was another way out.

"Like what?" Hut said. "I don't want to get killed."

"You could go to Mexico," Bancroft said.

It's too bad guys like Bancroft don't all go somewhere and stop degrading the legal profession in this country.

Another thing Judge Osborne did that any cop would approve: He kept that complicated preliminary moving right along and got it all over in the two weeks planned. Most of our Beverly Hills judges would have let it hang on twice as long by allowing irresponsible objections and delaying tactics.

George Slye, who was Jerry Chesterfield's attorney, would sit at the defense table and say, "Objection," when there was no possible ground for it.

"Overruled," Judge Osborne would say.

Now Slye would get to his feet and start with a peculiar gesture he has, kind of pointing at the judge with the forefinger and the little finger of his left hand extended like a two-pronged fork, and he would say, "But, Your Honor. . . ."

And the judge would interrupt him. "Counsel," he would say, "I have overruled you. Now let's get on with the case."

That happened several times, and Georgie didn't like it very well; it surprised him because he is used to getting his way in Beverly Hills. But by the end of the first day in William Osborne's court every attorney there knew who was the boss.

Maybe a year later I happened to talk with Judge Osborne at a baseball game on Catalina, and this bit with Georgie Slye came up.

"Yes," the judge said, "I know all about that little clique in Beverly Hills. But I'm not beholden to any of them."

The preliminary came to an end on a Friday night, but only because Judge Osborne made it end then. The defense was still trying to nitpick and drag things out, and Gregg Marcus was going on vacation the next day and had his airplane reservations for his family and his plans all made. And the defense wanted to put everything over to Monday.

You'd think that would suit Judge Osborne fine because he had to fly in from Catalina every morning and fly back every afternoon, and if he couldn't get home before dark, he had to stay in a hotel overnight because there are no night landing facilities on Catalina.

But the judge said, "Mr. Marcus has his vacation plans all made, and I don't think it's asking too much of the rest of us to remain here until eight o'clock or so tonight and finish this matter. In fact, I'm going to call a five-minute recess right now and go call my wife and tell her I won't be home."

There's a lot more to running a court than knowing statute law and case law. There are ten thousand little things, like Judge Osborne's consideration for Gregg Marcus' personal problem, and his skepticism about George Bancroft's argument for bail for Hut, and his impatience with the courtroom billiards of a hustler like George Slye. Go into Judge Osborne's court and watch the wheels turn, and you will see the machinery running the way it was intended to run; it's one of the most impressive things you'll ever see.

After the preliminary was over, about seven o'clock that Friday night, Judge Osborne hung around in the courtroom talking, probably because he had no place to go but a hotel room. He came over to where Gregg and I were getting our stuff together, and he said to Gregg, "Why didn't you file on all eighteen cases?"

"I was limited to five, Your Honor," Gregg said.

"Well, it's too bad," the judge said. "You could easily have won all eighteen."

When we went to trial in Superior Court downtown, we got a different kind of judge entirely, Billie Ann Howard. Judge Howard means well, but she doesn't know criminals and she doesn't know enough law, and any smart defense attorney can con her. The only reason we got convictions was because we could bull our way past her with overwhelming evidence.

It's a curious coincidence, but two months after my kidnap-rape-robbery cases against Jim Grimes were filed and pending, this same Judge Howard dismissed an almost identical LAPD kidnap-rape-robbery case against the same Jim Grimes on the ground of judicial error in the preliminary hearing.

She may have been right about the error, but she was wrong about the way she handled the dismissal.

Bob Knight, the deputy DA who prosecuted the LAPD case, told me that Grimes' attorney was already in chambers with Judge Howard when he got there, and she never gave him a chance to object or argue. She just told him she was dismissing the charge.

"I might have consolidated the cases," Bob said, "but I was never given a chance. The ruling was prearranged, worked out in advance, and I was closed out."

So LAPD took its case into Judge Howard's court and lost. Mine went into Judge William Drake's court, and Grimes went to prison. That kind of discrepancy raises questions about judicial competence that are never asked and never answered.

For a while Georgie Slye had the same inside track with Judge Howard that Grimes' attorney did. Every morning, it seemed like, Georgie would have a cozy little visit with the judge in her chambers, and they would talk and drink coffee, just the two of them without the presence of Jim Pregerson, the deputy DA on the case.

I talked to Jim about it. I said, "Jim, it's unethical. I'm pretty sure the state bar would frown upon it. One more time, and I'm going to stand up in open court and talk about it, and she can throw me in jail if she wants to."

So Jim went back and complained to the judge in her chambers, and she sent her clerk out to talk to the lawyers privately and tell them that nobody was to have coffee with the judge unless the other side was there, too.

After which Georgie Slye came over to the prosecution table—it was during recess—and said to me, "Lynn, I know where that came from. Why are you raising so much hell about me going in and having coffee with the judge? What's wrong with that?"

And I said, "What's wrong with that, Georgie, is the same thing that's wrong if it was Jim Pregerson in there having coffee with the judge without you. It's unethical as hell." A cop could see it, but Georgie couldn't, and neither could Judge Howard until I threatened to embarrass her about it.

One of the first things she did in the trial was throw out an important piece of evidence, a letter to Comstock from Sandy Showers in which she was worrying about driving him on these rip-offs and what might happen if he was caught. We found the letter in the apartment, under a search warrant, so Judge Howard couldn't throw it out for illegal search and seizure.

She threw the letter out because it might prejudice the jury against the defendants! We're trying to play an honest game, and the judge is dealing jokers. Hell, on the basis of her argument you could never convict anybody of anything because all the prosecution evidence would always get thrown out. It was one of the weirdest rulings I ever heard of.

A little later everybody spent a day in suspense while the lawyers argued about one juror who didn't show up that morning. It turned out that during the night he went out and got himself busted for robbery.

I don't know what difference it made that the guy was a crook; all it proved was that C & H and Co. were being tried by a jury of their peers. Anyway, the trial went on with an alternate juror.

But everything came to a crash stop when LAPD Detective Del Baker got on the witness stand. He told how C & H were under LAPD surveillance for two months, long before we busted them.

"Now why were they under surveillance?" Georgie asked. "Unless, of course, you had already made up your mind that they were guilty." He knew damned well why they were under surveillance, and he was trying to get it into the record so he could object and claim prejudice.

Del said, "They were under surveillance because they were arrested and convicted for the same kind of crime in this same area seven years ago."

"Objection! Move for mistrial!"

Judge Howard put her head in her hands, which was leading the jury if anything was, and called the lawyers back into her chambers.

After a while Jim Pregerson came staggering back out like a baseball player who had just been beaned at the plate. "Goddammit!" he said. "I can't believe it at all! I have never even heard of anything like it!"

"What happened?" I said.

He said, "She is going to come back out and get up on the bench and tell the jury that what Del Baker testified is not true. I can't believe it!"

What it meant was that the judge was deliberately going to lie to the jury; she was going to commit perjury in her own court! Del and I were both madder than a cotton moccasin that's just been stepped on.

"I'm not going to let her get away with it," he said. "I'm going to tell the jury."

"Great!" I said. "I'll stand up to let my position be known, and I'll say something, too, if necessary."

"She'll probably jail us for contempt," Del said. "But the hell with it!"

So Judge Howard came out and perjured herself, and then Del stood up in the witness stand and I stood up at the counsel table, and Del said, "Ladies and gentleman of the jury, the court is trying to mislead you. I was in on the arrest in 1967 of these suspects."

Now both Judge Howard and Georgie Slye covered their heads with their hands, and it was back to chambers again.

When they came out again, the judge told the jury that what Del said was "partially true," which was partially a lie, and then she declared a mistrial because the jury had heard the truth!

It was the same old story. Several of the jurors came up to me afterward, and every one of them said something like, "I don't understand it, Mr. Franklin. How can she declare a mistrial if it's true?"

I felt like kicking the courthouse down because I had no answer.

The next day both Del and I went down to the bank, and we each drew out $550 cash to carry at all times, because the judge had told Jim Pregerson that she was thinking of citing us for contempt. We were going for a new trial, no question, and we might need that money, which is the cash bail for contempt.

A lot of things happened as we got into the new trial. Sandy Showers, who had not been able to remember anything because she was trying to protect Comstock, found herself a new boyfriend and suddenly developed total recall. We made a deal, we dropped all the charges against her, and she turned state's witness.

When that happened, Bill Ringer gave up and copped out: He pleaded guilty to four robberies.

And Georgie Slye, running scared now, managed to get Jerry Chesterfield's trial for receiving separated from the others. He figured his client would look better going it alone; he wouldn't seem to be so closely associated with C & H.

Comstock and Hut were punch-drunk but still fighting, and their attorneys managed to get a few days' delay, which gave Jim Pregerson and me a chance to look into something. We had continually discussed how these guys could take $1,200,000 worth of jewelry and continue to live in that $125-a-month rathole on Hacienda. They didn't go out and hit the night spots, they didn't spend money wining and dining, they didn't blow it on clothes, and the only travel they did was one trip to Hawaii that Comstock and Sandy made. We couldn't figure where the money went.

Neither could Sandy. "Lynn," she said, "you tell me they took more than a million dollars' worth of jewelry, but I just can't buy it. They didn't have any money. Why, I even bought all the groceries out of my airline pay, and a couple of times I had to buy underwear for Comstock. They just didn't *have* the kind of money you're talking about."

Jim and I kept kicking that around.

"There's *got* to be some buried money or some buried jewelry, something," I said.

"I agree," Jim said. "But where do we look?"

I thought about it and said, "Look, nobody has talked to that guy that hired them up near Fresno. We've got a little time here; why don't we go see him?"

"You're on!" Jim said.

So we drove up Fresno way to see Howard Stanton. He was a guy maybe sixty, and he had a little old ramshackle house on about four acres, and half a dozen beat-up trucks that he kept cannibalizing to keep some of them running, and a ratty trailer where C & H stayed when they were up there. It was a fringe operation, hauling cottonseed and fruit mostly; he was not getting rich.

We settled down with the guy and his wife for some coffee, and we told him we wanted to look over his employment records about C & H. It was all friendly, but Jim surprised me; he worked with me just like another cop would. I'd ask a question, and before Stanton could get over any confusion, Jim would bore in with another that backed him up. Jim was the first DA I ever knew that might make a good cop, too.

"Is there any place around here where they might have stashed away any jewelry or money?" Jim said.

"No," Stanton said, "I don't know where it would be. They lived in that trailer out there in the yard, but they couldn't hide anything there."

"Could they have buried it?" I said.

"Could be," he said. "But they're pretty busy when they're up here. Not much time to go around digging holes. But you're welcome to look if you want."

We looked at that bleak four acres, and we weren't ready for that yet.

"They're pretty busy here, huh?" Jim said.

"That Hut, I've never seen a harder worker," Stanton said. "Long hours, heavy labor don't bother him; he keeps right at it until the job's done. Now Comstock, he's lazy. But he's always having fun, when he's not sleeping in the trailer. You know, it's funny about those ski masks, because one night a bunch of the boys was sitting around in the headlights of their trucks, waiting to load up, and suddenly here comes somebody running out of the dark wear-

ing a ski mask and yelling up a fright. And then he laughs
and pulls off the mask, and it's Comstock. He laughed his
head off."

I said, "Mr. Stanton, how about the money he loaned
you?"

There was complete silence. I had struck something. Finally, he said, "Well, it wasn't all that much."

Jim came back quick with, "We have over a million-
dollar loss here, Mr. Stanton, and there's got to be quite a
bit of it somewhere. *How* much?"

"Well," he said, "not that much, but I have records of
whatever amount it was."

I said, "Could we see the records?"

So he told his wife to get out the deposit slips for the bank
account, and we started going through them. The first thing
we found was a deposit of $5,500 just two days after the
Harmon Bellows robbery, where they took $5,500 in cash,
hundred-dollar bills, off the top of Harmon's dresser.

"What's this money?" I said.

"That's Comstock and Hut's, really," he said. "They
didn't have an account, so we put it in my account. It
bought the truck that Comstock drives, but it's registered
to me."

And that was how we found out about the $5,500; it was
just a shot in the dark. When I asked about the money,
Stanton could have said, "What money?" and we wouldn't
have found anything.

The truck was a GMC tractor, an old one with a new motor; it was a big rig, just like Hut's, and Stanton owned the
trailers they pulled. It turned out Hut had worked for Stanton several years ago, before we sent them to prison the first
time, and he bought a truck then. After they got out of prison, and they picked up the $5,500, Hut arranged for Stanton
to buy Comstock a truck, too.

Two guys just out of prison awhile, and putting up all
that cash, Stanton had to suspect something was wrong.
But he wasn't involved in the robberies in any way; he's a

hardworking guy who got a little larcenous and made a little mistake. So instead of making a case out of it and maybe getting nowhere, we made a deal with him. He signed a note to Harmon Bellows for $5,500, at 7 percent interest, and he is paying it off at $250 a month until he can sell the trucks and pay it all. He has already made several of those monthly payments.

With the Stanton truck deal out in the open, Hut recalculated his chances and threw in the towel. He copped out to the whole thing. But Comstock fought all the way.

"It's a psychological thing," he told me after the trial when I visited him out at the prison in Chino. "Word gets around fast in a prison. If you've been a snitch, if you've cooperated with the police, you're a no good son of a bitch. And if you give up halfway through, you're a weakling. I knew that I was going to spend probably ten years in prison, and I wanted the people I was going to have to live with for ten years to *know* I don't give up. So I made you prove that I don't."

"Okay," I said, "tell me another thing. Why did you switch to robbery? It was always burglary before."

"It's more of a sure thing," he said. "I decided we were always going to go in when the people are home and wake them up. If you go in at four or five in the morning, that's when a person is sleeping their soundest; there's less chance of panic. And if the people are there, the jewelry is there unless it's in the bank. If the people are out of the house, maybe they're wearing the jewelry."

It wasn't bad thinking; it reminded me a little of the way Ben Colt thought.

The only case we lost was Dr. Weir's, which gave the goddamned DA downtown an .800 batting average against the ski-mask bandits. I hope that made him happy. Dr. Weir lost his own case for us because he demanded respect but he didn't give it. We worried about him as a witness right from the start, in the preliminary.

I talked to him before he went on the stand. "Dr. Weir," I

said, "for the sake of your own case don't get up there and let them get you uptight, don't get offended, and don't make the jury mad at you. Work with us on this."

He promised to try, and the first thing he blew it. Comstock had an attorney, Morris Brentlin, a guy with long hair and a beard who was noted for handling narcotics cases, and Dr. Weir didn't approve of him. Brentlin used this, he used Dr. Weir's attitude, he played him like Al Hirt plays a horn, and he got exactly the jazz he wanted.

Dr. Weir got on the stand, looked at Brentlin and said, "What are you doing on a case like this? You only handle narcotics addicts."

And the judge had to interrupt him and tell him to be respectful.

Then Brentlin called him *"Mr.* Weir." He did it deliberately.

"Dr. Weir," the doctor said.

And Brentlin said, "Excuse me, Doctor."

"I've been a doctor for forty years," the doctor went on, like a snapping turtle. "I respect the title. Don't con me. Don't be sarcastic. I'm stating a fact."

The judge was getting a kick out of all this, and he put in, "You have it coming, Mr. Brentlin."

But Dr. Weir couldn't let it alone; he kept talking. "Suppose somebody addressed you as 'Ditchdigger,'" he said to Brentlin.

And Brentlin said, "Do you think 'mister' is a ditchdigger?"

Now the judge was getting fed up with this bickering, which had nothing to do with the case. "You are getting sidetracked, Mr. Brentlin," he warned.

And still Dr. Weir kept gnawing at it. "I think your comment is entirely uncalled for," he said to Brentlin. "I corrected you twice."

"Excuse me, Doctor," Brentlin said for a second time.

The judge tried to cool off the doctor. He said, "Mr. Brentlin is required to be courteous, Doctor, and he will be. I'm sure it won't happen again."

"I'm not used to using the term 'Doctor,' " Brentlin said. And he said, "Excuse me," for the third time.

"I think you are," Dr. Weir said. He still wanted to argue; he just couldn't drop the subject.

"Let's cut it off right there," the judge said, getting mad as hell now. "Put your next question, Mr. Brentlin."

About twenty of those caterwauling incidents in the final trial soured the jury. They didn't give a damn about Dr. Weir's robbery; they just wanted to put the shaft to him. And they did; they found the defendants not guilty in his case.

But they convicted them on every other charge, and we put them away. C & H each got ten to life; Ringer got a year in county jail. The charges against Sandy Showers were dismissed at our request, after she testified for us. And if there ever was something going between her and Comstock, her testimony put an end to it.

When she left the witness stand, she walked close to him going back to her seat, and he said, "How do you feel now, Officer Showers?"

What we had left now was the receiving charge against Jerry Chesterfield. Ringer had told us that Chesterfield admitted to him in jail that he made up the story about getting the jewels from Jack Silver for appraisal, and Ringer testified to that.

So Georgie Slye had to change the story. He put himself on the witness stand and said Chesterfield had admitted to him that he got them from C & H, and he claimed Chesterfield didn't even know C & H before the night of the bust.

Which was just another perjury. Out at Chino, Comstock said, "Hell, it was Sean Hanratty that introduced us to Chesterfield back in 1972. And Sean tells me the guy has been fencing at least since 1966."

250 of your ski-mask stuff did he receive?" I

"How much of your ski-mask stuff did he receive?" I
said.

Comstock said, "All of it. He told us what to look for, he
said, 'Nothing but diamonds; don't bother with anything
else,' He handled all of it."

I said, "What did he pay you for it?"

"About seventy thousand," he said.

"About sixty thousand," Hut said at the same time.

They looked at each other, and Comstock said, "Well,
somewhere in there."

"Are you sure that's all?" I said.

"We got no reason to con you now," Comstock said.

"But the loot from the eighteen jobs was one million two-
hundred thousand dollars retail value," I said. "What the
hell happened to the rest of it?"

"I don't know," he said. "Chesterfield says it wasn't that
much. He was always telling us that most of it was junk
jewelry."

Chesterfield was still hollering, "Junk!" about the stuff
he got from the Jonathan St. Cloud job, but the court's
official appraisal was $24,600, which is pretty classy junk.
It was amazing; here the guy had spent his entire life in the
jewelry business, he had testified about jewelry and diamonds in many legal cases as a recognized authority, and he
hung onto that story like it was the last lifeboat leaving the
Titanic.

So I said to C & H, "I think you are the guys that really
got ripped off."

Slye on the trail of a fat fee had all the ethics of a mon-
goose in heat. First he collected a $25,000 fee from Ches-
terfield, and then after a while he got up in court and told
Judge Billie Ann Howard that his client had run out of
funds, and he asked to be appointed by the court to repre-
sent Chesterfield at the taxpayers' expense. Judge Howard
said okay.

Meanwhile, I had been looking around, and I found that
right after he got arrested, this penniless old man went out

and bought himself a new car for cash. He paid for it in full with a check.

So I went down to his bank on Wilshire, and I found that he had a safe-deposit box there, as well as the account. The bank people aren't supposed to tell you things like that, but if you work them right, they will.

So we went to Judge Howard and got a search warrant for the box, and I told Georgie Slye to have the old man there to open it or we'd torch it.

Georgie said, "You won't find anything. He has told me the box is empty." Georgie never quits, I'll give him that.

Chesterfield came down and opened the box with everybody witnessing, and in it we found 196 pieces of jewelry, which we had officially appraised at more than $119,000. None of it was ski-mask loot, but we did get one piece identified as stolen somewhere else.

Next, I found a savings account of Chesterfield's at Home Savings and Loan, and it had more than $50,000 in it. During the previous year, when he was supposed to have had no income at all, he made three deposits, one of them for $8,000. The story at the trial was that the $8,000 was the payback on a loan he had made to his son.

So here we had a guy that was worth about $170,000, and he was pleading poverty so the public would pay his legal bills. Jim Pregerson got up and asked Judge Howard to set aside her ruling that Georgie Slye was Chesterfield's court-appointed lawyer.

And Slye said something like, "Well, Your Honor, I was never actually appointed. I wish to apprize the court of the fact that I would never take any money from the people to defend Jerry." He always called Chesterfield by his first name.

Jim pointed to the court record, which showed that Slye was wrong; he *was* officially appointed.

And Slye said, "Yes, but we never did make a declaration of assets, so the appointment is invalid."

Judge Howard agreed. But her ruling was not the correct

one, which would be that the appointment was made, but its qualifications were never fulfilled. She ruled that she *never made* the appointment. Aside from her disregard for truth, you have to wonder how much law a judge like that really knows.

All this flimflam, perjury and assorted varieties of deceit didn't fool the jury; they convicted the bastard.

There was a little time before sentencing, which in California is a separate court proceeding. The main reason was so the Probation Department had time to make a report and recommendation to the judge. The report filled the judge in on all the stuff that did not come out in the trial because the jury was supposed to be kept in ignorance, like the fact that Chesterfield received $1,200,000 worth of jewelry.

While we were waiting for the hearing, I took that same information to the Internal Revenue Service, along with the information about his $50,000 savings account and the $119,000 in jewelry in his safe-deposit box.

And they said, "We have no case pending against Jerry Chesterfield. We can't do anything."

"Start one," I said. "Here's your evidence."

"Sorry," the guy said.

"Look," I said, "if I was delinquent in my tax or if I failed to report something, you'd sure as hell jump all over me. Now how about jumping on somebody else?"

And he said, "We can't do it. Unless we have a case pending, since Watergate we can't open a new file."

I never found out why, and I don't believe that Watergate bull anyway; what the hell has Watergate got to do with it? But they wouldn't move on it.

The California Franchise Tax Board would. This is the state's little IRS, and they jumped on it faster than a hobo hopping a fast freight one step ahead of a Burlington cinder dick. They took that $1,200,000 figure at face value, and they slapped a due bill on Chesterfield for $121,927.38 in taxes, interest and penalties, and they clamped a lien on his

$119,000 in jewels and made me their agent responsible for holding the stuff.

An FTB guy came around to see me and asked, "How did you find out about this?"

I said, "I found out he bought a new car."

And he said, "Oh, he owns a new car, too? We'll tie up the car!" There was a guy who was enthusiastic about his work. Maybe the IRS should turn its entire operation over to the California FTB; we might pay off the national debt.

The probation officer in his report quoted Chesterfield: "I have heart trouble, prostate trouble, and a herniated disc and emphysema. I feel that I would die if I were sent to jail. My wife is very ill and I do not believe she will be able to survive if I am not able to be with her."

And the PO summed up this heart-rending information by saying, "The defendant cries a good deal."

Then he said, "It is very unlikely he could have been as naïve as his explanation of his behavior would have one believe. His principal motivation for his involvement was probably greed and criminal opportunism. He was a vital link in a criminal chain from crime to disposal of the loot."

And finally he said, "The defendant's connection with a gang whose total activity involved vicious robbery-burglaries over an extended period of time has not been diminished by his sorry family and personal circumstances. These are not mitigating factors to his crime. There appear to be no extenuating circumstances."

And the guy recommended that Chesterfield get a jail sentence and probation.

Judge Howard read this report, she mulled it over, and when the time came to pronounce sentence, she laid on Jerry Chesterfield a fine of $1000 and straight probation. Not a day in jail, not one!

After twenty years of winning cases in the street and losing them in court, that was the straw that broke this cop's back.

Here was a guy who fenced $1,200,000 in jewels in eleven months. He paid C & H, take the high estimate, $70,000. He paid Georgie Slye $25,000. He paid a fine of $1,000. Those are his total expenses.

Just add it up. A fence sells jewelry for half the wholesale price, or one-quarter the retail, which in Chesterfield's case came to $300,000, round figures. Subtract his expenses, and his net profit for eleven months came to $204,000. And unless the California FTB collects something, which is doubtful, it was all tax free!

"Don't ever tell me crime doesn't pay," Jim Pregerson said while we were picking up our notes and official papers off the counsel table.

"Oh, hell, Jim," I said, "let's face it. We lost the war against crime in the courts years ago. The people just don't know it yet."

When I walked out of that courtroom, I walked out of police work, too. I quit it for the rest of my life. And if I could have slammed the door behind me, I would have.

But the goddamned courtroom door has one of those shock-absorber gadgets that won't let you slam it. It closed very quietly.